RADICAL SELF-LOVE

Live a Vibrant Life Beyond Limitation and Fear

NIKI HUGHES

www.radicalselflovebook.com

Radical Self-Love: *Live a Vibrant Life Beyond Fear and Limitation*

Niki Hughes

ISBN: 978-1-7388943-0-7

Cover Design: Pankaj Singh Renu

Edited by: Tamelynda Lux

First Printing Edition 2023

Three Graces Publishing
PO Box 112, Stn Main Saanichton,
British Columbia, V8M 2C3 Canada

Niki Hughes is available for individual sessions, group sessions, and customized workshops and training.
Call (236) 237-0038 or email Niki at
Niki@elementalbalance.ca for booking information.
www.elementalbalance.ca
www.radicalselflovebook.com

Why Read This Book

Do you feel an ache of emptiness inside, like something important is missing? Do you yearn to feel loved—by you? Do you crave a better life where you can feel your vitality and value? If you want to live from your expanded, loving heart like the superstar of your own life, this book is for you.

If you want to come first, feel deep appreciation and love for everything about you, and step into your vibrant life, **radical self-love** is what you need.

Young or old, it's never too early or too late to find and live in a place of **radical self-love**.

In the pages ahead, you will take a journey to free yourself from what blocks and limits access to your own beautiful heart—your true self. I have you reach inside to discover your own worthiness and dive into the deep well of love, appreciation, and support that opens up everything in your life.

This book is a step-by-step guide to returning to your true self, where you can live within the incredible love your heart and soul hold for you. And when you do that, everything changes in beautiful ways.

If you are ready (and I know you are), this is your book.

About the Author

Niki Hughes is a certified hypnotherapist, BLAST trauma practitioner, energy healer, empowerment coach, and meditation and mindfulness teacher, in private practice on Vancouver Island in North Saanich, British Columbia, Canada. Niki is the creator and former radio show host of the *Past Life Explorers Show,* which aired on the News for the Soul network.

As a heart-centered healer and change agent, Niki has worked with hundreds of people to help them thrive through change, enabling them to live more connected, abundant, joyful lives by igniting their divine inner spark and stepping into personal empowerment.

Niki provides her hypnotherapy and coaching services in person or over the internet and serves clients worldwide.

When not helping others thrive through life change, Niki will usually be found creating something beautiful in her garden or hiking the west coast forests and beaches with her family and spunky little dog, Lily Puggle.

Would you like to work with Niki? Niki is available for 1:1 coaching, hypnotherapy, spiritual hypnosis sessions, meditation and mindfulness training, group sessions, custom training classes, and workshops.
Call (236) 237-0038, visit **www.elementalbalance.ca,** or
email niki@elementalbalance.ca to set up a free consultation.

What Others Are Saying About This Book

"This is valuable information for anyone feeling stuck in life. This book will help you fall in love with yourself, overcome your limits, and connect to your highest purpose."

~ Joseph Hoyt, author of *A Fruitful Life*

"Radical Self-Love is a powerful book and another example of Niki's ability to help us tap into the human spirit and become better people. For those ready to build a better life and live from self-love, this book will be your GPS."

~ Susan Simmons, world record-holding pioneer adventure swimmer and inspirational speaker

"Most everyone experiences self-doubt, uncertainty, and fear, often without understanding where such feelings originate from. *Radical Self-Love* helps readers uncover their origins and provides tools and strategies to push them toward bigger, better outcomes. It's a must-read for anyone who wants to live an authentic, heart-centered life!"

~ David Knapp-Fisher, speaker and author of *Punch Failure in the Face, Then Buy It a Beer*

Dedication

This book is dedicated to all who are waking up to the simple truth that loving yourself is the most important action you can take.

For Jenna, Jordan, Shannon, and Mila—you are my greatest treasures, my greatest joy, and my greatest teachers. May you always live an uplifted life and shine the light of your radical self-love into this world.

Acknowledgments

I have been blessed with many incredible teachers in my life, for which I am eternally grateful. For those who have had the heart and courage to step out into this world and share their wisdom, teach, and inspire others to learn and grow, I thank you from the bottom of my heart. The world is a better place because of the gifts you give.

Table of Contents

Chapter 1

Your Power Source: Radical Self-Love Is Your Key

"To know thyself is the beginning of wisdom."
– Socrates

"I must get to radical self-love, and I don't have much time." The subject line of the email was steeped in urgency. My curiosity and interest heightened, I opened the email and read on. "I've been diagnosed with stage 4 breast cancer, and I want to live what time I have left to the fullest. I need to get to self-love and let go of the fear of loving myself. I've had two rounds of breast cancer already, and I've started treatment now for the third, and I need to feel love and acceptance for myself so that I can leave here whole. Can you help me?"

Honestly, I was a little stunned at both the directness and the challenges this woman Marina, was facing. I've never had a client specifically ask to work on self-love, especially without the luxury of time to get there. Of course, this is where we end up for many of my clients, but it isn't our typical entry point.

Marina was in a dire situation and knew something had to change. She also knew the change had to be hers. Having tried many things over the years to feel better, she was ready to go to the source now and improve and expand the relationship she had with herself.

As I finished reading her email, I knew I would help Marina. I was just hoping she had enough time left to get there.

How much time do YOU have?

The truth is, when it comes to opening yourself to the most powerful love there is—self-love—you don't have any time to waste.

In the mid-400s BC, the famous philosopher Socrates said, "To know thyself is the beginning of wisdom." You must find out who you really are to understand yourself, your character, and your limitations. It's through self-knowledge that self-mastery is born, enhancing the ability to live a purposeful and fulfilling life. You can't love what you don't know, so when you know all the aspects of who you are, the opportunity to change, master, and radically love yourself becomes present.

What is radical self-love? It is a feeling and an action. Self-love can be defined as recognizing and appreciating your inner worth and value. I think of self-love as the deep connection to the part of you that is warm, strong, loving, and just *knows* who you are, *knows* what you are capable of, and accepts every single thing about you. It lives in your own heart. Radical self-love lives in this wonderful, supportive, and empowered place, and it creates confidence in putting yourself first in everything you do.

This deep level of love, the love you have for yourself, impacts everything in your life. How you feel about yourself affects your health, wealth, relationships, and everything in between. It impacts the *vibrance* of your life and how good it feels across all aspects of your life. Vibrant living will be different for me than it is for you, your family, or your neighbor down the road. It's a personal state of goodness.

For me, my vibrant life is elevated, connected, and creative; it is flow, ease, and lightness. It is joy, and it is sparkle. It's **magic!** And when I feel these things, I know I am living in radical self-love, creating my vibrant (shiny!) life. It just feels, well, easy.

What does a vibrant life mean to you?

I first met Leanna when she came to see me about some physical problems related to her weight. She was losing weight rapidly and didn't know what the issue was. Her medical team was unable to come up with a reason or diagnosis for the weight loss, so she wanted to do some hypnosis work with me to understand and clear whatever was in her way. Leanna was fifty-five, had left a twenty-five-year abusive marriage a few short years before, and had three grown children. Her son had stopped speaking to her a year before coming to see me because he didn't approve of or appreciate the romantic relationship she was in with (another) difficult man.

Leanna experienced trauma early in her life. She felt abandoned as an infant by her father when he walked out on the family and then by her mother, who was not present for Leanna because she had six kids to care for on her own. As a young child, Leanna was put outside alone to play and had little nurturing interaction with her mother, who Leanna said did love her but was hanging on by a fraying thread, trying to manage life on her own. Leanna was raised by her older siblings, who weren't equipped to do the job.

Leanna's younger life and programming created a deep sense of lack. She had low self-worth and self-esteem, which resulted in little love or confidence in herself. She grew up, left home, and spent her life in a series of dysfunctional and abusive relationships. She said she felt "invisible" and was challenged to speak up and advocate for herself. In her current situation, Leanna was with an emotionally "unavailable" partner who didn't treat her very well. She felt this relationship and situation were better than nothing and, at this time, was necessary for financial reasons. Her important family relationships were suffering, her physical body was suffering, and she was stuck financially. Leanne knew she wanted better for her relationships, physical body, and financial health.

Self-love is the foundation of a great life; it is the program that underpins everything. Leanna recognized that her self-love was low to nonexistent, resulting in her being stuck and unhappy, with the negative impacts of her choices playing out across all areas of her life.

Leanna wanted more for herself, her health, and her family.

We worked together to release the unresolved trauma of abandonment from her childhood and all the fears created as a result that were lodged deep in her body. She felt invisible as a child and believed she "wasn't important" and had to be "small and quiet." Her whole body was wrapped up in being small and quiet. With the stress in her current romantic relationship, she came to understand that her body was doing just that: becoming small and quiet by losing weight.

Leanna reset her negative limitations and reprogrammed herself into "I am standing tall and empowered" and "I am whole. I am enough." She came to embrace her courage, fearlessness, confidence, and her own value. "I am just as worthy as everyone else," she said. Leanna felt free, and she connected with her own heart. She felt self-appreciation, self-worth, and, most importantly, self-love.

A few weeks later, when Leanna and I finished working together, she was on an upward trajectory. She found better work, changed her living situation, and was working on a plan to end the relationship she was in. She reconciled with her son and was hopeful this would make them stronger. She stopped playing small, and the weight loss leveled off. She emailed me to say, "I feel stronger, I feel grateful, and I know in my heart I am enough."

If it's so important, why aren't you just born in love with yourself?

Well, the short answer is you are. As a newborn baby you were open-hearted, connected, and expected great things. Yes, you! And then life threw you some curveballs. Throughout your life experiences—the trials, the traumas, the wounding, the pains, the interactions with others—you got pushed away from yourself, your heart, from your spirit. Layers upon layers of protection were built up. Those layers stop the harsh external world from getting to your most vulnerable place, but it also stops YOU from getting there too.

Your personal programming and the stories created by those difficult moments will help you in the short term to survive, but over time, unchanged, the programming, stories, and protections become a significant impediment.

The layers that you set up to protect you eventually block and disconnect you.

You might wonder why does it matter? Well, that disconnection leads to all kinds of difficulty and struggle. If you don't have love for yourself, your self-worth, self-esteem, self-confidence, and self-appreciation suffers, which means you struggle with many aspects of your life. You may struggle with your weight, have bad romantic relationships or friendships, or be in a job that doesn't fulfill you. You may feel directionless. Life may just feel like you are pushing a big old heavy boulder up a hill. There is no flow, no ease, and you feel high stress in your everyday life. And it feels like if you were to let go, if you move a muscle in any direction, you would be crushed by that boulder rolling back on you.

When you are living blocked and disconnected from yourself, you live in a lower *frequency* or vibration, and everything around you in your world is operating at that same low frequency too.

Celia Louise writes in *The Champagne Chakra*, "You are a living energy field, and everything (every atom, every object, every living thing) is in constant motion, vibrating at a specific frequency. In humans we understand this as an individual's rhythm or energetic pattern." You have a unique energy pattern that you can control and change.

Think of your life as a mirror. That mirror reflects to you what you are sending out into it. What it reflects is based on your energetic pattern or frequency, which means the things you see, feel, and attract into your life match the frequency you are sending out. Send out joy and get joy back. Send out anger, get anger back.

The mirror reflects a life that shows how you feel about yourself, how you talk to yourself, your mindset, your limitations, your stuck emotions, and all the "stuff" that you carry in your energy field. The life picture that is reflected to you is based on YOU.

When you have self-awareness and take the time to clean up what you are sending into your mirror, you will get a cleaned-up higher response back. It will match the new you. The more you clean up what you put into your mirror (your life), the better the reflection will be.

Sometimes it's hard to recognize or be aware of where you sit and even to take stock of how you feel about yourself. I know I was so busy dealing with life, pushing that boulder up the hill, and moving from crisis to crisis that I didn't have TIME to consider where I was or how I felt.

A good many years ago, I was in *another* heated argument with my (soon-to-be-ex) husband. As our relationship unraveled, this was a pretty standard moment, with both of us in rather loud defensive modes protecting our positions and getting nowhere other than to drag each other through the mud one more time. My anger was most definitely leading this one, and as I was on my verbal roll in the middle of this day's tirade, he yelled back at me, "You know what your problem is? You really don't love yourself very much." And with that, he turned and stomped away. Ouch! Talk about a fight-stopper. That kind of comment was so out of character and out of left field that it felt like a glass of ice-cold water was thrown in my face. I was speechless, which was unusual for me at that point in my life, and it forced me to go inside myself to see if I had an answer.

Did I not love myself? Of course I did, I think. I assumed I did. I started to tick the boxes in my mind: I was a good person (tick!), I was successful (tick!), I was getting a TON of things done every single day (tick!), I was a good mom (tick!), most people liked me (tick!) . . . and then as I was building this mental list, I paused, and defensiveness stepped in screaming at me, *How dare he make this about me!* And I let myself be distracted, and away it went. I was back to the anger, back to being right.

And yet, in that moment of self-inquiry, before I started defending myself, the truth was I had absolutely no idea how I felt about myself. I had spent my entire life up to that point looking at things outside myself as my measure of happiness and validation of how "good" I was. I completely lived up to the expectations of others, always trying to exceed them, and I lived off my to-do list, which was incredibly long. The funny thing about that to-do list was that there wasn't anything on it that was nurturing for me. When I returned to this thought later, the truth was I was severely disconnected from the real me. I was completely separated from my own heart, and it wasn't a very happy place to be, and it was showing.

My personal journey into the awareness of self-love had begun. Now I just needed to figure out how to navigate and get myself onto the right roads.

What I discovered was to find your way back to your deep well of self-love, the layers and programming that cut you off **must go.**

Just about every issue I see in my private practice comes down to a struggle with the sense of worthiness and love for self. When you put yourself at the back of the line, the bottom of the pile, that's where you will stay. Invisible and unseen.

Often when people come to see me, it's because they've had what I call a "wake-up call from the universe"—a trauma, a debilitating physical illness, an accident of some kind, or a scary unplanned life change, like losing a job or being handed divorce papers. The wake-up call gets you to stop for a minute and look at yourself. It's an opportunity to assess how you got to this moment and understand who you really are and what you truly want for your life.

When you struggle with loving yourself, **everything struggles**—jobs, people, situations, opportunities, relationships, and so much more. Like that mirror, all the pieces of life get reflected to you at the level (or frequency) you are operating on. If it's high, you will see and experience high-frequency life. If it's low, you will see and experience low-frequency life. To elevate your life, you have to "up" your frequency. Cultivating self-love is a fast way to pull yourself into a higher level of living.

The good news is when you shift and peel away the layers to open yourself up to your own value and love, everything changes. Your frequency naturally lifts. You feel positive about life. You live in a greater state of harmony and flow. You feel worthy and respect yourself. Your resilience grows, and you can handle life's bumps and stresses much easier. You have a better sense of direction in your life. Your relationships improve. You smile more. And best of all, **you *feel* a deep appreciation for yourself** that radiates outward, affecting everything in your life.

Peeling away the layers isn't a terribly hard thing to do. It may feel overwhelming when you start, but like anything new, you take it one step at a time—one layer at a time, one program at a time—and you will surprise yourself with how quickly you can get the job done. To step into self-love, you have to let go of the wounds, pains, traumas, and negatives that hold you back to allow your light to shine inside you and through you out into the world.

Are you wondering what happened to Marina? Marina and I worked together for a few months peeling away the layers holding her back. When she came to her first session with me, she said her number one goal was to "fall in love with myself again" so she could enjoy the time she had left after her cancer diagnosis and impending treatments. She was enthusiastic about getting going and was excited at the prospect of feeling herself again.

When she was young, Marina was a quiet child, introverted and self-sufficient. She never asked for anything and never rocked the boat. All her life, Marina went with the flow, never speaking up or advocating for herself. She never married and never had children, and at her current age of sixty, she found social situations difficult and had difficulty speaking up. She found them so hard that she avoided them and hadn't gone out or seen friends for some time. Marina had trauma and negative beliefs, severely limiting her ability to love and feel loved. There was a lot to unpack.

After our second session, where we cleared negative beliefs, Marina came to my office and was radiant. She stood taller and was bubbling with excitement. She couldn't wait to tell me she had met a man and was going on a date. "I feel like a teenager again!" she exclaimed and then proceeded to tell me that she had some great conversations with old friends and was meeting one for a walk the next day.

As a hypnotherapist, trauma practitioner, and energy healer, I've seen and worked with a lot. A lot of trauma and wounds, a lot of blocks, and a lot of people who are down, stuck, and disconnected from themselves. I've helped hundreds of people create change and shift into a higher vibration of living where they experience their own value, open up, and get stronger in their foundation of love for themselves. You can too.

When you let go of the past, the stories, the traumas, the wounds, and the programming, you take a beautiful step into the deep well of love and appreciation for yourself. When you make loving yourself your first priority and put yourself at the top of your list, everything around you changes. You lift your frequency to a higher playing field and then life unfolds in beautiful ways.

I've written this book as a map back to yourself, a journey through the layers back to your heart and soul. And by virtue of taking the journey to rediscover that beautiful place and putting your self-love first, you will return to who you were truly meant to be and live a life of radical wholeness.

I invite you to find your radical self-love and learn to put yourself first in the chapters ahead. You can follow along chapter by chapter and use the ideas and tools to uncover and let go of what holds you back, or you can chapter surf and move through the chapters in a way that feels right for you. I know that when you follow the ideas and use the tools presented here, you will shed the old programs and let go of old blocks so that you can step into your goodness again.

As you take the journey, you might find that some of your wounding is big or overwhelming. If you are dealing with serious, complex trauma, post-traumatic stress disorder (PTSD), or mental health issues, please reach out and find assistance to help you through the process of clearing and letting go. Talk with a compassionate friend, a counselor, a hypnotherapist, or a healer to help you. (You can find my contact information at the back of this book if you would like to work with me.) **Be compassionate with yourself**. Rome wasn't built in a day, and you don't need to go fast if what you really need is to go slow. Be as kind to yourself as you would be if you were helping a dear friend work through their healing process.

Along the way, I share stories hoping that you will see how ordinary people like us have transformed. Some stories are from clients, and I share some of my story and path back through my own difficulty, trauma, and wounding. These stories are meant to help you feel empowered to take the steps outlined to find your way home to loving yourself and changing everything, and I mean *everything*—for a more fulfilling and enriched life.

The tools on the pages ahead are tools that I use in my practice and that I've used for myself. I share the authors/teachers/ healers I learned these from as resources for you should you want to dive deeper to continue your learning and healing journey.

I've created **free bonus resources** for you to accompany this book: meditations, affirmations, and self-care tools. The free bonus materials for **Radical Self-Love** are available for you to download at www.radicalselflovebook.com

No two journeys are alike, and some of the things I cover in the pages ahead will resonate with you, and maybe some won't. Connect with what works for you, and let the rest go. It's that easy. Really!

One of my favorite quotes I love to share is, "The mind, once stretched by a new idea, never returns to its original dimensions," by Ralph Waldo Emerson. I promise you will stretch your mind with the ideas and tools in the pages ahead, and if you take the journey with me to the end, a new and more loving you will emerge.

Think about these questions or journal on them as you prepare to start your journey:

- **What is my biggest challenge in taking the journey to radical self-love?**
- **What are the best ways I can support myself on this journey into radical self-love?**
- **What will be different in my life when I am living from radical self-love?**

I'm going to ask you that difficult yet important question again. **How much time do you have?** I don't know your timeline, whether you will make ***this*** moment the moment for change or if you will make it a week or a month from now. I do know there is an urgency for all of us to get ourselves back to radical self-love and to allow that high-frequency feeling to propel us forward in life—in wholeness. It will move you in ways you never imagined.

Chapter 2

The Barriers to Your Inner Heart

"Allow things to come and go,
keeping your heart as open as the sky."
– Lao Tzu

"She's had a massive deep stroke, and your mom may not make it. The next twenty-four hours will be crucial." My mom's husband gave us the devastating news that Mom collapsed on a trip and was in a hospital four hundred kilometers away. Mom was under treatment for metastatic breast cancer, and a stroke was something for which I hadn't prepared. At all. Our lives would never be the same again, especially Mom's. She would live six more years in care, unable to speak and walk and care for herself independently.

Mom was a beautiful person inside and out, and she was the ultimate mother. She had many lifelong friends and was considered the "Life of the party." Everyone loved her. Even the friends I went to elementary school with all those years later at her funeral had wonderful things to say about my mom. They remembered her forty years later! She was effervescent. Joyful. She loved music, danced, and was a talented artist; for the three of us kids, she was our fun, hip, loving mom who would do anything for us. And she did. The problem was my mom was a huge giver—she gave and gave and rarely put herself first. Honestly, it would have to be something of massive proportions for her to speak up and take action for herself.

Some of those times happened. After thirty-plus years, she left her marriage to strike out on her own. At that point, she had NEVER lived on her own; she had gone straight from her own mom's house directly into married life. After her divorce, she wasn't alone long, and she quickly fell into the role of caretaker and "giver" with husband number two without much thought about herself.

I don't remember Mom ever doing any deep internal work on herself, looking inside to let go of life's baggage and connect to authentic self-love. Through her divorce, I know her confidence and self-esteem grew, but I never saw her reach the place of radical self-love.

The side effect? Over the years, an underlying anger grew inside her, quite contained and below the surface, but it reared up occasionally. As she aged, she became a little more irritable and had a little bit shorter of a fuse. The anger became a little easier to see. I came to recognize the expression in her eyes and the slight shift in the tone of her voice when she agreed to something she didn't really want to do. It was just a tiny flicker across the eyes, and then bam! She locked it down. There was nothing radical about self-love there!

I'm glad she got to make changes in her life so she could feel empowered and in charge of her own life. Unfortunately, the years and patterns of putting everyone ahead of herself, cutting herself off from self-love, and the low-level anger seething underneath her cheerful (and beautiful) smile created devastating physical issues. She experienced breast cancer at fifty-nine, a second round of it at sixty-seven, and in the end, a debilitating stroke at sixty-nine that took her to an early death at seventy-five.

The change process is hard, especially when the change is in your inner world, pushing on your identity. Who am I if I'm loving myself and putting myself first? It takes great strength to rise and move beyond everything you know in order to be true to yourself. Sometimes that little voice in your head saying, "Something has to change; this doesn't feel good," just isn't enough to motivate this kind of change. It takes *action.* And sometimes, the inaction of leaving yourself in your comfort zone feels better (in the moment, anyway), and at least there, you have a good idea of what's expected of you, right?

Identity level change means you must have the gumption to go in and (gently) peel yourself apart, or at least clear out the gunk that's in your way. If you've been telling yourself you're not good enough, or you're a bad person, or you don't deserve goodness in your life, that's a heck of a lot to step over. Even if you have the awareness that you need to get to radical self-love *and* the willingness to do it, you still need to know *how* to move yourself forward and then take *action.*

Knowledge is important. Just don't let yourself stop there.

Personally, I am a serial book buyer and learner. I love to learn and I love books! What I discovered many years ago is that the knowledge I was collecting was certainly interesting, but what I was gaining from all my exploration and reading had limits. As one of Tony Robbins' famous quotes says, "Knowledge is not power. Knowledge is potential power. Action is power." I recognized that I had to take action to make that knowledge become anything useful to me.

As my mom used to say, "You can lead a horse to water, but you can't make it drink." Experience trumps knowledge any day in my world. It's the action that makes the difference.

What gets in your way?

Brace yourself. The biggest issue you face is yourself. Whaaaat?? Can you believe I said that? Yes, it's YOU! You are your biggest issue. Not your partner, not your job, not your kids, not your bank balance. Your mind, what you think, what you feel or don't feel, and how you choose to react create your biggest issues. You know from experience you can talk yourself into most anything and talk yourself out of anything too.

When things are uncomfortable, which do you do?

The awareness of what you are doing is one of the basic issues you face in getting into radical self-love. You need to know when you are cut off, how you feel, and where you would rather be.

Getting to radical self-love requires that change comes from within you, not from outside of you. No matter what changes happen outside of yourself, you will still be left with the crappy feeling of being disconnected. Why? Because you haven't cleared your way back in.

When you are out of self-love, out of alignment with who you were meant to be, you can consider yourself to be *afoul* of yourself.

To run afoul means you are in conflict or difficulty with yourself. Being out of love with yourself is the biggest difficulty you can have with yourself and your life! Let's dig in a bit and see just how afoul you are.

AFOUL is: Awareness, Fear, Others, Unhooked, and Limitations

Awareness: Being without awareness means just that: You are bumping along in life without realizing that life could be so much better and all your situations could be improved. In fact, without awareness, your situations may get worse. You are accepting the status quo and setting yourself up for more of the same or worse. Awareness lets you RISE. Awareness shows you something needs to change.

Fear: Fear created from wounding and traumas lodged in your body as blocks keep you separated from so much, from self-love and the creation of a confident life with forward momentum. Fear creates uncertainty, doubt, and a lack of trust—in others and in yourself. It can make you afraid to look inside and afraid of change. Fear tricks you into believing the status quo and standing still is safe.

Others: Blame others for your challenges and life issues with no responsibility for yourself and the quality of your life, and you will stay stuck. A challenge with blaming others is that being a victim is so easy! Absolutely nothing is required of you if you can point your finger somewhere else. With "others," the thought is, "It can't be me. Someone/something else is creating this."

Unhooked: Being unhooked means being disconnected from your emotions. When something uncomfortable shows up, if you can't handle it (or don't want to), you shove it down deep inside and suppress it. There are many reasons we do this (hint: see earlier). Distraction is another way of disconnecting from your feelings, which in the end, is disconnecting from yourself. There are a multitude of ways to distract yourself from feeling: alcohol, drugs, overworking, food, and being terminally busy. Living a life of disconnection from feelings may work in the short term, but you need a healthy relationship with your feelings to navigate life and feel self-love. For "unhooked," you get: "It doesn't feel good, so I am going to ignore it."

Limitations: Your beliefs are the programs that help you get through life. Beliefs can either support you in life or hold you back. Core beliefs, the really deep ones, are generally created in childhood and, for the most part, keep running until you do or experience something to change them. The beliefs that **limit you** in some way or *stop* you from something are based on fear. And guess what? From your beliefs come patterns of behavior that reinforce the belief. You guessed it, a limiting belief or set of limiting beliefs creates a negative pattern. Getting trapped in a cycle of negative patterns and limitations is another way of creating separation from yourself. Limitations tell you, "I have to stay small to operate in my world."

When you run AFOUL of yourself, and trust me, you only need one of these to be offside with yourself, **you invite powerlessness in**. You step off the innate power that radical self-love brings, and life suffers.

Stop for a moment and think about where you are.

How am I running AFOUL of myself?

What is in my way of making change?

Life without self-love is a difficult one. Without change, you will continue in the same vein and bypass positive, enriching, and empowering growth. Staying trapped in victim-ness, fear, and limitations means you maintain more of the same, and even worse, more drama, chaos, pain, wounding, fear, and negativity are present. Your filter shifts and your reality is painted with negativity, making it hard to cope. Your resilience takes a beating, and your relationships suffer. Depression, anxiety, and stress take a strong hold, and your body starts to suffer. Even though she kept smiling, my mom's spiral downward was physical—from cancer to stroke to death.

"I'm ugly, and I'm not important." We were halfway through our session around limitations when Marina "found" this limitation from her childhood. There it was. It just popped to the surface for her to see and examine. She felt she wasn't lovable, worthy, or useful.

Marina had gone through two rounds of cancer treatment, holding onto these big limiting beliefs and fears. She had a deep fear for her safety and a devastating rejection in school that made her "give up trying" at a young age. And now, as she headed into her third round of breast cancer treatment, her awareness was high. She knew it was her work to do, and she was ready and willing to dive in and let go of it all.

Something inside Marina pointed her to look at herself and get to radical self-love. The good news is Marina was listening—her awareness was ON, and she took responsibility to clear out what was in her way.

I'm happy to report (and I'm sure Marina is too) that she's still with us over two years later. Cancer treatment is behind her, and she is living a heart-centered, self-love-filled life. She started dating and met a lovely man. She brought new healthy, supportive friends into her life, now speaks up and advocates for herself and what is good for her and is socially active out in the world.

How many times have you doubted yourself or kept quiet in a conversation? How often have you just gone along with a request because it was *easier*, even when you had a terrible feeling about it somewhere in your body?

You are not alone.

A study done by Ipsos in 2020 showed that one in two women worldwide feels **more self-doubt than self-love**. This is half the population of women **globally**, which is astounding. This is not just a female issue, I might add. I know that a high percentage of men feel disconnected and lack love for themselves too.

Facing your fears and seeing your limitations can be terrifying. Let self-compassion support you. I thought I was okay with myself until that moment when my self-love was questioned. Until then, I hadn't given it any thought at all. I was too busy. I knew I was proud of my accomplishments, my intelligence, and my contributions. I had pretty good self-esteem, but I always had this little niggly disquieted block over my heart that I continually chose to ignore.

Here's how it went for me:

It's easier not to.

I don't want to look at that!

I'm too busy. I have too much to do. I'll do it later.

I'm too tired (because I have too much to do).

I'm a good person, isn't that enough?

If you have been telling yourself these things, I understand. I had many opportunities to get out of my own way before my big "thump on the head" awareness moment happened, but I didn't. It could wait. I could wait. Other things were more important. Other things came first (I certainly didn't). If you can't interrupt yourself and the way you are living, you will face bigger challenges. The stakes will become higher as the part of you that needs you to reconnect—your heart and soul—creates even bigger moments that might capture your attention and wake you up to what's required in your life. My mom ignored her moments and ended up in irreversible physical decline.

What could be more important than discovering the deep well of love and appreciation waiting for you? From discovering how amazing you are? From discovering how important you are in this world and in your own life? And from operating from this place of strength and love?

Nothing really. But I know timing is everything, and the perfect time presents itself when you are ready. And if you aren't, it will ask again. And it will get louder, and the stakes will go higher. I ask you, are you ready?

If you are, I want you to know a few important things.

Know that <u>you are not broken</u>. Life is an experiential journey of learning, healing, and growing, and healing our wounds is something every single one of us faces.

Know that <u>you can clear the way to radical self-love and</u> put yourself first so that your life flourishes.

Know that <u>you are not alone</u>. This is a journey that all of us who want a better life for ourselves will take.

Know that <u>you have everything you need</u> to step into radical self-love.

Know that you can do this in small pieces if that feels right for you. You don't need to do a complete overhaul of everything in twenty-four hours. You can take it as fast or slow as you want.

Know that you are never too old to reach your own heart, live from the heart, and improve your circumstances through self-love.

The tools in this book will help you to uncover and let go of what keeps you stuck. This discovery can be made on your own, or if you want to work with a professional, you can do that too. Just do what is in your best interests, and you will already put self-love into action.

Chapter 3

The Map to Your True Self

"Self-love is not selfish; you cannot truly love another until you know how to love yourself."

– Unknown

While it may feel daunting to turn the headlamp on and peer into your dark places, this particular mining expedition doesn't have to be years in the making and fraught with pain and suffering. It can be quick, and believe it or not, it can feel good! That's because what needs to be released, changed, and let go of is often at the surface, interfering with your life.

"I don't know why I'm so angry; it just seems to come from nowhere, and I'm reacting to the littlest things. I'm pissed off all the time, and I don't know what's wrong with me." Helen was caring for her aging spouse, who was transforming from a vital entrepreneurial man into someone who needed more and more care each day. "I am a happy person. This is so unlike me. I need to get this fixed!"

I'd known Helen for about a year and was helping her on her healing journey. I knew her to be curious, inquisitive, and open but never angry. Something was rising to the surface that needed addressing quickly.

Sometimes it's that obvious, and sometimes it's not.

With every step you take toward yourself, a certain level of "rearranging" will occur. Helen's changed circumstances with her husband's health meant the internal *rearranging* was underway, and in her case, it loosened something angry to look at and let go of.

Whether large or small, each step allows you to see yourself in a better light. A positive light. A radiant light. Every layer you peel and cast off will bring you closer to the golden prize, your own heart's light, and the steadfast, compassionate appreciation for all you've experienced that got you to this incredible moment and for who you are allowing yourself to become. Really.

For Helen, she discovered her anger was based on fear. In her past, fear had created the negative pattern of walking away when times got tough. She was determined to see this through, which meant facing that fear and letting it go.

There are many ways to move down this road of healing and change. The most important thing is that you move, are curious, and allow change. There are many "tried and true" ways of getting on that road of change that I use professionally and personally. Everything in this book is something I have done for myself, and let me tell you, I have done a *lot* of healing work over the years. So much so that I barely recognize the *me* of a mere five years earlier.

Depending on how far away you are from your true self, your beautiful heart, and radical self-love, you may need some of the strategies presented here or all of them. Regardless, think of these strategies as the map and the fuel for your journey.

1) **Wake Up to Where You Are**

Are you aware of your mindset? Are you a positive or negatively focused person? Becoming aware of your mindset and understanding your mindset creates everything in your life is a major step to radical self-love. It's worth repeating, so here goes: **You are the creator of everything in your life**. Don't panic, and don't feel bad if you're standing in a mess. It's never too late to get started and realize that you are in charge of YOU and that mess you made can be cleaned up into the life you want.

Accepting that you're in charge of your own reactions, decisions, thoughts, and ultimately your own life is **awareness,** and that awareness opens the door to choice.

It's never too late to stop bumping along at the whim of whatever happens around you. Trust me, I was in my early forties when I figured it out for myself, and I still don't have it all perfect. Earlier on in my life, I was great at blaming others for my drama and unhappiness. I was always looking externally for the cause. And then I had the magic of awareness wake me up, and the door of choice was right in front of me.

With choice comes the awareness of **actively** managing your mindset to elevate your power and create a higher frequency of living. From there, more good things come.

This understanding of awareness and frequency changed everything for me. It meant I had to stop blaming others for the challenges in my life, and that wasn't always easy.

There are always going to be challenges. I firmly believe we are here to experience a large variety of challenges to help us grow, learn, and become better people. With awareness and a managed mindset, you can then make the conscious choice of how to step up to those challenges based on what you want for your life.

You get to choose. So will it be a positive choice to help your life expand in good ways or a negative one that keeps you stuck?

2) **Hug Your Past and Let It Go**

Yes, I did mean hug. There is a lot to be learned about who you are *and* the amazing inner resources you have gained from the things you've been through. As horrific as those situations and events may have been, there is learning when you can set that part aside and look underneath. Even if the learning is, "My god, I never want to do that again!" That's an important message for you and will shape the forward motion of your life. When you can acknowledge the good bits, it's easier to let go of the bad bits.

Fear is underneath all the traumas, wounds, blocks, and the ways in which you limit yourself. I've heard people say, "Fear isn't real," or that "Fear is **F**alse **E**vidence **A**ppearing **R**eal." I can tell you the feeling of fear, especially fear in the moment, is completely real! While *anticipated* fear may not be real (the thing you fear hasn't happened yet), the feeling in your body is completely real. In fact, that fear feeling can stop you dead in your tracks.

You need a certain level of fear to live a healthy (and long) life. It's designed to keep you safe, to stop you from stepping off a cliff or jumping out of an airplane without a parachute. Imagine if you had *no* fear. How long would you last in this world? Probably not long. I think back on my life, and those times fear held me back (for good reason), and that healthy dose of fear was my friend. I'm still here.

The challenge comes when fear becomes unbalanced and it blocks you. Fear blocks are the feeling inside that keeps you stuck or unable to even take a step. It's tight. It's unreasonable. You want to get beyond it, but it feels impossible.

Trauma, negative emotional events (wounding), and difficult situations create these fear blocks on the inside and tightness in your energy field and life.

Your challenge will be to decide if you will let fear and your past stop you, or will you say "Thanks for the learning" and move past it?

3) **Un-Limit Yourself**

If that isn't enough, the mind, which is a meaning-making machine, creates beliefs about who you are and how you fit into the world. If these beliefs are created from fear, it's only natural they will limit you, right? "I'm not good enough," "I don't deserve nice things," "I'm unworthy of love."

From there, the mind looks for evidence of those beliefs and sets up negative patterns. Have you noticed that when one toxic friend leaves your life, another toxic friend shows up? Or a bad partner? They just keep repeating because of this limitation in you that says, "I'm not worthy."

It's a vicious cycle that keeps you trapped, cut off from your own heart, and fully loving yourself where you live in a lower frequency of life than you need to.

Address the fear, the limitations they create, and the patterns you are living to let yourself rise to a new, higher, and more connected level.

4) **Make Friends with Your Emotions**

It may not feel like it, but your emotions are your friends, or at the very least, they should be. When you ignore these "friends," they hang out in the background, just waiting for an opportunity to rush in with full force, screaming, "I'm here, I'm *here*, I'm HERE!" Then you end up overwhelmed by them. If you've been giving these friends too much of your time, they are probably sitting in the driver's seat, running your show. When those friends are difficult, say angry or jealous, it can make your life perfectly hellish. Just like you would with the people in your life, you need to sort out who are your good friends and let the bad ones go.

Your emotions are with you to guide you. In theory, yes, it's that simple—does this feel good, or does this feel bad? And then, let's do more of the good feeling stuff and less of the bad feeling stuff. It certainly sounds easy, but in reality, it can be much harder to manage than that.

Making friends with your emotions means you let your emotions in, accept their goodness, and then let them go. The emotions you may have been ignoring or suppressing need a compassionate escape, a way to come up so you can acknowledge them and then send them on their way.

Mindfulness lets you get to know your emotions without becoming entangled with them. When you are mindful and can observe what's coming up in you with curiosity and compassion, you can stay out of analysis and judgment. And then they go.

Emotions are here to help you, even if it doesn't feel like it. Knowing how to allow and become friends with your emotions means that as you get their love messages and let them go, you clear space inside you for something better. All that clutter of unprocessed emotion clears, and you become better connected to your heart, and self-love can move in.

Mindfully allow the emotions that need to get out of the way of self-love to rise from that scary dark place and move on their way.

5) **Embrace Your Positive Qualities**

It's no surprise that as we all grow up, we are shaped by our experiences of people, situations, and events. This shaping is where you create inner resources, talents, and skills. These may be obvious to you, like your ability to play the trumpet, or not so obvious, like your incredible resilience because of all the difficult life circumstances you have navigated and changed.

These are your positive qualities.

Everyone has their list; for some, this list is long, and for others, it is incredibly short. Short lists (or even no list that you can think of) don't mean a "less-than" life performance so far. It just means that the list is hiding in a deep place. It hasn't been brought to the surface to be acknowledged and worked with yet.

Using your positive qualities to affirm who you are and how you want to show up in the world is a powerful way to move from self-criticism to self-acceptance. Self-acceptance feeds self-love.

Your positive qualities are your GPS back to radical self-love. When you build your list and grow these qualities, you close the gap between no self-love and radical self-love.

6) **Be Radical, Put Yourself First**

This is the essence of radical self-love. Knowing you are important enough and you matter enough **to be first** in your life is empowering. If you don't know yourself or don't have a strong awareness of who you are and what you want, I'm guessing you probably find yourself second, third, or plain old last on the list of life's priorities.

You may have learned at an early age to mold yourself to others' expectations and desires and ignore your own. Yet when you make yourself and your wants, desires, and needs a **consistent** priority, you are honoring yourself and who you came here to be. Your heart opens.

Putting yourself first is an action of self-care, and self-care is a vital part of loving yourself. Self-care can be expressed in many ways and will be unique to you based on your circumstances and needs. It may be a daily walk, a special coffee, or creating your dream vacation. You send a message of kindness and self-compassion to yourself, and in turn, you get to know yourself better through self-focus and nurturing.

Boundaries are the lines you draw around yourself and others that express your needs. Without boundaries, others won't know where the lines are, and through your interactions, you may end up feeling taken advantage of, put out, unappreciated, and ultimately last on the list. A lack of boundaries creates anger. Create that boundary, the line that "Shall not be crossed," and you send a message to yourself and the people around you that "I matter." And then you do.

Boundaries are essential to putting yourself first (or, in some cases, on the list at all) and are a necessary and empowering part of your self-care.

7) Go Beyond, Build Your Higher Connection

I've got news for you: the *thing* you've been searching for to fill the empty feeling inside is the connection back to yourself. Yes, it's back to you again! So many of my clients (and some friends) talk about the *emptiness* inside, the *hole* inside, the *aloneness* they feel, and I can tell you that getting yourself back to YOU is how you fill it.

Maybe you've spent a good part of your life seeking and searching for the THING. Look externally to fill that space (relationships, food, drugs, alcohol, to name a few), and you will never come to your own wholeness. Your wholeness comes from inside you, from tapping into your own heart and soul to activate self-love. Taking this step further makes it **radical self-love** when you open up to the larger part of you, referred to as your Higher Self.

Your Higher Self has your back. Your Higher Self knows everything about you and loves you unconditionally. Yes, for **all of it**. Every mistake, every success. Your Higher Self is your only true partner and best cheerleader.

Connect to your Higher Self, build and nurture that relationship, and radical self-love is sealed.

There is a way forward. These seven strategies will help you to create deep change and allow you to reclaim yourself. To elevate yourself. To find a bigger version of yourself. To love yourself. What are you waiting for?

Chapter 4

Wake Up to Where You Are

"The mind is everything. What you think you become."
– Buddha

Mindset is defined as the "established set of attitudes" held by someone. Your mindset, how and what you think, feel, and believe, creates your attitudes and is critical to making your way back to radical self-love. It's impossible to feel loving toward yourself if your mindset doesn't support it.

Do you run on autopilot, or are you aware of your mindset? Do you recognize when you go down into a negative spin? Are you a positive or negative person? Where do you spend your time most days?

"I've lost everything good in my life, and I'm just about to lose the last of it." Kathy was living in a spiral of despair and negativity, and after years of blaming others for her miseries and disregard for herself, she was about to bottom out.

In her sixties, Kathy had yet to develop a strong sense of awareness. She told me when she started out in life, she was positive. She had great parents, some difficult siblings, and a pretty good school experience. Social and sibling challenges happened, and without awareness, she was in blame and judgment with a massive serving of both heaped on herself. Kathy's extremely negative mindset and victim-ness grew. She felt she was a failure, "pathetic" was her word. There was no self-love, and she was nearly completely disconnected from herself. By this time, she was disconnected from just about everything else too. Her family didn't speak to her. All but two friends had walked away. She lost her job the year before and was running out of money and would soon have nowhere to live.

Without awareness, Kathy blindly went down a negative road that continued to grow like a black grimy rolling snowball. Every step she took down that road was a step further away from herself and her loving heart.

Kathy struggled to open to the awareness that she was responsible for what she had created with her life, and she had to take action to turn it around. Thank goodness the part of her that wanted to create something better reached out for help. I knew that for Kathy to move from self-loathing to self-loving, it would be a big job, and we would start at ground zero with awareness and mindset.

You are the creator of everything in your life.

Oh, how I know that one hurts. How could you possibly be responsible for the bad things happening to you, right? It was hard for Kathy to come to terms with, but she got there. Like Kathy, you are in charge of your reactions, decisions, thoughts, paths to travel, and, ultimately, your life. No one else is unless you are under the age of majority or live in an autocratic society. When you accept this, you become **aware.** When you become aware—of the things around you, the feelings within you, and how you choose to show up and interact—that awareness opens the doors of choice.

Don't panic or feel bad if you're standing in a big steaming mess. "I can't believe what a horror show I've made of my life," Kathy said, "I'm so pathetic." In those small moments when she was taking some level of responsibility, Kathy got busy attacking and mentally punishing herself. She couldn't see the forest for the trees, let alone a path she could move forward on. So she stood still. For years. Mired in negativity and blame, constantly undermining herself, she closed her eyes to herself and the situations that were occurring. "It's not me. It can't be me. There's nothing I can do." Rather than **wake up—become aware, shift her mindset, and lift herself up**—she took the absolute teeny, tiniest slice of responsibility for the life implosion that was happening. The good news was that a teeny tiny bit of responsibility had the awareness to know something had to change.

Awareness is your opening.

In the book *The EQ Edge* by Steven Stein and Howard Book, they describe (self) awareness as "The ability to recognize your feelings, to differentiate between them, to know why you are feeling these feelings, and to recognize the impact your feelings have on others around you." I would take it a few steps further and include the recognition of the impact you are having on yourself and your life. What you don't recognize, you can't manage, and when you don't manage, you don't make good life decisions, like our friend Kathy.

Awareness is **always** the precursor to change. If you are not aware, then there is nothing to change, is there?

Awareness is your opening and your opportunity to change mindsets.

With awareness, you can check in on your mindset and change what needs to be changed. "Where am I right now?" is the big question, and "Is it a positive place or a negative place?" It's an important question because it indicates how you are showing up to life. Kathy showed up metaphorically decked out head to toe in an entirely negative outfit, including accessories.

When you can look at yourself and see how you are dressing for the party called *life*, you can then decide it looks good on you or not. And then change outfits.

A positive mindset is connecting. It's your natural state. It's easier to live in, and it's where life feels good. When I tell you it's connecting, I mean it connects you to the larger part of you. It's in your heart. This larger part of you is supportive and wise, has your back, and is incredibly hard to connect to and notice from the negative place. A positive mindset takes you there, and lifts you *up*. It elevates you.

A negative mindset is separating. If your natural state is to be positive, being negative means pushing yourself farther away and separating yourself from your own well of love, from your own heart. A negative mindset does no lifting. It keeps you right where you are, or even worse; it drops you down as it was with Kathy, down and down and sometimes into a complete downward spiral.

The choice is yours. Would you rather lift *up*, closer to your natural state of worthiness and love, or spiral *down* further away?

A few decades ago, when I was first made aware that I was the creator of what I was living through—my negative, victim mindset—it was like an electrical shock jolted through my body. A giant ZAP. My world turned upside down while I processed this foreign concept. Just before that knowledge came in, I knew I was unhappy and a little bit angry, but I also truly believed it was because of what "they" were doing. *It can't be me. It can't be, it can't be me. What if it's true? What if it really IS me?* was gathering steam as it rolled through my shocked mind while I sorted through what this really meant to me, to my life. I was highly capable. I was super responsible. I was navigating the immense chaos in my life, and I was still keeping it together—another ZAP. I was uber-responsible at responding to situations and events, but I was simply reacting. I wasn't aware of or managing the inner me through the process. I wasn't happy a lot of the time, I didn't feel joy, and I didn't realize it yet, but I was out of love with myself (I could only do one epiphany at a time). My mindset was becoming more negative than positive. That was about to change.

Rise Up with Frequency

Your mindset is a key component to the move into radical self-love as it is a significant contributor to your personal frequency.

Let's get down to basics. At the very core of everything is energy. Your energy is your life force, and like all things energetic, it has a frequency or vibration. Every molecule, every cell is spinning and vibrating. This creates a specific frequency, and just as every "thing" has a frequency, so do all the bits and pieces of you. All those bits and pieces vibrating within you add up to your *home* frequency.

Have you ever met someone and just felt they were *off*? Or listened to someone speak and felt you couldn't connect with what they were saying? Your frequencies don't match; they don't resonate. What about the people you meet who feel like you've known them your whole life? They feel incredible to be around. Your energetic frequency is in alignment.

Where you are in your home frequency says a lot about your mental state, your attitudes, what you think and believe, and your physical state too. If you've ever had to hang out or live with someone who is *down* or negative (low or lower frequency than you), you will know that their energy and mental attitudes can impact yours. It's hard to be around a lot of negativity and not be affected by it.

The other side, of course, is when you are with people who are *up* and positive (higher frequency than you), you are uplifted in your energy, and it feels really good!

Let's think of life as an apartment building, and today in your current mindset and home frequency, you are living on the fourth floor. The first-floor folks have a lovely, functional space with one bedroom, a galley kitchen, and no deck. The fourth floor where you are is much nicer, and it has a bigger kitchen, an extra bedroom, and a deck off the living room.

The penthouse on the fifteenth floor of this building is stunning. It has four bedrooms, an office, a media room, floor-to-ceiling glass windows with a panoramic ocean view, a wraparound deck with a built-in barbeque, and brand-new modern furniture. It's all your favorite colors too. This is the place of your dreams.

Floors five through fourteen are all incrementally better and offer something new and desirable.

Your vibrant life is in that penthouse, but from the fourth floor, it seems out of reach.

How to get there?

Like in life, the key to lifting up (to that penthouse, your dream place) is to raise your frequency. As your frequency rises, you move to the next floor, or if you do it well, maybe you skip a few floors and go even higher. Each apartment gets more and more beautiful with better perks and amenities, and then, voila! One day, you have arrived. The penthouse is yours.

Lifting yourself to a higher frequency or vibration of living changes everything. It connects you to your core state of love, where you can access the larger part of you, where radical self-love lives.

Frequency is affected by the environment, other people, what you eat, but most importantly, by what you think, believe, and your **emotional state of mind**. Love is the highest frequency emotion and, because of that, is the most important frequency changer. Self-love is the most consistent and expanding love of all; it's with you always, and when you are living in it, you are guaranteed to be at a higher frequency of living.

Awareness + Mindset = Frequency, which, when you lift it, moves you closer to the true you, your heart, and the joys of radical self-love.

Kathy could have continued to just keep doing what she was doing, blaming, ignoring, and punishing herself, continuing her downward spiral of negativity, but she knew this wasn't going to get her where she needed to go. She wanted to feel good, solve her problems, and come out of them feeling love for herself.

Don't you too? Look inside now and ask yourself, "**What needs to change to move my mindset?"** Is it a ground-zero change activating or fine-tuning your awareness? Is it moving from a negative to a positive mindset? Are you ready to move on up to that penthouse? I will show you some easy ways to get started using your awareness to understand where you are and how to shift and then lift into where you want to be.

Become Aware of Where You Are

Your mindset is your key.

To become aware of your mindset, first look to your past to understand your reactions and attitudes to situations, people, and events and how you respond to yourself.

- **Are you a positive or negative person?**
- **Are there situations, people, or events that shift you into a less positive mindset?**
- **Are you compassionate with yourself or hard on yourself?**

Use this discovery and then notice where you are in the moment.

The harder of these is the "in the moment" awareness. It's much easier to see what's happened when it's behind you. You can move yourself to in-the-moment awareness using intention, which, according to one of my incredible hypnosis teachers Mike Mandel, is "putting your will behind what you do." Set your intention to notice your mindset; before you know it, you will recognize the mindset or *frame* you are operating from in any given moment.

Next, enlist the help of your unconscious mind to assist you not only in noticing but then to help shift you to where you really want to be.

Enlist the Unconscious Mind to Help

The unconscious mind uses what's called the **reticular activating system** (RAS), a network of neurons in the brain stem, to filter out an enormous amount of information (twenty million bits) down to what the conscious mind can handle in any given moment (between five and nine). That's a powerful filter! What goes into that filter is what your conscious mind becomes aware of.

If you have ever bought a car, remember the moment of driving it off the lot and noticing that same car everywhere. When I bought my car, I remember thinking, *Did everyone buy this same car today?* since there were soooo many of them. They were always there, but that program wasn't in my filter yet, so I wasn't aware of them.

The car is an example of a happy and positive focus; however, if you are focused on something you don't want, that goes into the filter too.

The teacher at the front of our grade three class announced that our class contribution to the school's spring concert would be a musical medley based on the year's seasons. She said each season would be represented by a few of us dancing across the stage dressed *in season* and doing some seasonal highlight activity. I was already terrified. Shy, sensitive, and already feeling like I didn't fit in, I didn't want to dance across the stage in front of the whole school.

"You will all be dressed for your season," she said. In a flash, I saw *summer* and felt the panic rise as I imagined myself dancing across the stage in my bathing suit. I was in total fear now, feeling it in my chest; my heart was pounding as I imagined the horror of being in my bathing suit in front of three hundred students.

A hush fell over the class as she began assigning students to the parts. I dropped my head low, hoping upon hope not to be noticed. I chanted in my head, *not summer, not summer, not summer.* The teacher looked my way, and guess what? The terror was real because, with all that energy focused on summer, I was picked for it, and even worse, my summer partner was Ricky. From that moment on, the teasing ramped up: "Ricky, Niki, bathing suits." You get it. There's a lot a group of kids can do with that.

Had I known then what I know now about the unconscious mind, the power of focus, and how the RAS works, I would have focused on **what I wanted** (WINTER, WINTER, WINTER) and not what I didn't want (not SUMMER, not SUMMER, not SUMMER). The unconscious mind doesn't do negatives, so all it heard was my big emotion plus SUMMER, SUMMER, SUMMER. I was putting out the "I want summer" vibe, which was guaranteed to be mine. And yes, it was as bad as I thought (but I did it!).

The great news is by knowing how this works, you can use this programmable filter to have your unconscious mind work with you to create positive resources for you. By placing *things* into the filter, they come into your conscious awareness.

Mike Mandel has an excellent method to work with the programmable filter to fine-tune the RAS. He teaches you do this by asking the right kind of question out loud, which the unconscious mind then responds to. What you focus on fine-tunes the filter. How you formulate your *ask* (or request) of the unconscious mind is critical because the unconscious mind is just a big data processor. There is no discernment between good and bad; it's just going to offer you the information you asked for. Keep your questions framed in the positive, too, because the unconscious mind doesn't register negatives ("not SUMMER" turned into plain old "SUMMER"). The other thing you need to know about the unconscious mind is that it doesn't compute *time*. So always add the word "today" somewhere in your programming question to focus the unconscious mind on the current time. There is no point in bringing a resource to you in two years when you need it now.

Why Questions

Why questions will expand what you are asking about. For example, if you were to ask, "Why does this always happen to me?" or "Why does my life suck?" or "Why are people always treating me badly?" your unconscious mind, which doesn't discern and just processes the information you give it, will pop those why questions into your RAS. From there, all day long, you will see more evidence of "Why your life sucks" or whatever negative question you put out there. This is not a good way to bring you resources, so leave the WHY questions alone.

What Questions

What questions bring you options, almost like a big heaping smorgasbord. For example, you might ask, "What can I do to feel happy today?" The unconscious mind then brings you lots of resources of things you can do to feel happy. This is wonderful if you *want* lots of choices. The challenge with this type of question is that you can miss a lot because it's hard to notice it all, or it can be overwhelming. I say use this kind of question when you want a lot of options and are prepared to notice them all.

How Will I Questions

These are the best questions to ask because "How will I?" questions presuppose you are already there and creates a focused response. This becomes a nice, limited target for the unconscious mind. For example, "How will I have an amazing day today?" Your unconscious mind will show you an amazing day over and over. That makes your job of noticing so much easier.

If you want to become aware of your mindset, you can ask, **"How will I be aware of my mindset today?"** Nice and simple. The unconscious mind will create opportunities through the filter for you to become aware.

If you want to shift your mindset, you might ask, **"How will I move into a positive mindset today and have the awareness to recognize it?"** or **"How will I experience reacting in a positive way today?"**

Your job is to watch as these situations, opportunities, feelings, and reactions appear in your day. It's like a game. Cast a net with your questions and see what shows up. Put some emotion into it, get excited when you notice, and the unconscious mind brings you more.

Use this tool for awareness, mindset, or anything else you want to change or bring into your life. Remember to focus your questions positively and use the word "today" to set your timeframe.

There are no limits to how many questions you can ask. Remember, the unconscious mind is a super data processor, managing twenty million bits of information each moment, so you aren't going to overload it. A little warning, though: You can overload the conscious mind. In this game, the conscious mind must have enough power and ability to notice what you've asked for. I always recommend two or three questions to start so that you can build your awareness. Use the same ones each day until you have mastered them, and then change them up.

The Art of Reframing

Another way to move from negativity to positivity is awareness (recognize where you are) and then a reframe to shift that thought to take you to a better or more positive perspective.

A young woman called me not long ago to discuss an issue she had at work. She had recently left a work situation where she was being bullied and had just started a new job in a different field, in what she thought would be better aligned with her education and career goals. After going through the ten-day intensive training, she realized that this job would be more stressful than the last job, and it wasn't at all what she had thought it would be. It wasn't going to help her build her career, nor would it help her create skills to use in her chosen field.

When we chatted, she was upset and agitated at the thought of quitting this job. She saw quitting as *one more failure* to add to her growing list, and because of that, she was considering staying even though she would hate it.

When the stakes are high, and stress is in the mix, it's easy to get stuck in a narrow perspective. We had a reframing conversation that went something like this:

"I feel if I quit, then I am **failing one more time** at finding a job," she said.

I replied, "If it wasn't a failure, what would it be?"

"Well, it's learning, but it's still a failed job."

"Learning is important. We need to learn about ourselves, and this is how we do it—through experiences. What if it wasn't a failure but **just not a good fit**? For someone else with different skills, and different goals, this would be their dream job, right?"

"Yes, I guess it would be. It's definitely not mine!"

"And aren't the first few weeks of a new job and training really about assessing whether you can do the job, whether you are a fit for you and your bosses?"

There was a bit of silence while she digested this.

"Yes, you're right. If they didn't like me, if I didn't pass the training, they would let me go."

"So your bosses are looking for a fit too. It sounds like we agree. It's not a good fit. What happens if you leave this job?"

"I can find something that is a good fit."

"Yes, and you can keep at it until you find it, right? It's kind of like dating. You keep at it until you find someone that clicks. It's the same with jobs. It has to work for YOU. And what happens to the organization when you leave?"

"Well, I guess they get to find someone else that **is** a fit."

"Right! They want an employee who is happy to come to work, not super stressed, and is getting something wonderful for themselves from the work."

"Yes, it would be better for them."

"By staying in this job where you are not a fit, you're actually preventing the right person from having that experience and the organization from having a super employee."

"I owe it to them both to go!" she smiled.

She went to work the next morning feeling strong in her decision to leave and gave her two weeks' notice. We reframed her perspective of "failure to 'fit'" and the solution for her was clear, and she felt good about leaving that job.

I took a strange elective in high school that was only offered a handful of times. In a grade event forty years ago, this kind of class was not mainstream. It had ten students, was mainly discussion, had no exams, and was based on positive thinking. It taught me valuable skills about mindset that I have used my entire life. The teacher, Mr. Brooks, was a quiet man, and the rumor was he was either a priest before he was a high school teacher or a monk. I didn't care. I took this class because it was an elective and sounded easy. Of course, I was wrong, and it turned out to be mentally challenging. Mentally stimulating, actually, and it stretched my mind in some wonderful ways. This gifted teacher presented situations from the news that were negative, dire, or difficult and had us dive in and come up with as many positive aspects as possible. Through discussion, the class had to come up with meaningful reasons to be positive and flush out the impacts of the opposite perspective being portrayed in the media.

Mr. Brooks would pull something from the news, like "Riots Over Food Prices," and then, as a team, we would flip that into a provocative statement for discussion, "All food in grocery stores is free." From there, we would engage in creative discussion to understand the positive aspects and impacts. Negatives were completely off-limits because they are so much easier to see. Negative is our default as humans, and it turns out Mr. Brooks was trying to change that. We were encouraged to go WAY out there; if it was positive, no idea was off limits. It was a creative process that taught us to uncover positive perspectives and to see another side of difficult things. In teaching us this creative process and the ability to see another perspective, another angle, Mr. Brooks was teaching us to reframe.

When you reframe, you are opening yourself up to another perspective, just like Mr. Brooks did for an entire semester.

To reframe and open to a different perspective, find the thought or attitude you want to change and ask yourself:

- **How does this benefit me?**
- **How could this be positive?** or **What is positive about this?**
- **What does this mean to me, about me, or for me?**
- **What else could this mean that would benefit me?**

Being anxious or fearful is often based on the negative stories you tell yourself about your future. Those stories haven't happened. Your creative mind is putting you there, but it's just a story. Through awareness, you can recognize where you are—out in a negative future—and from there, you can move or

reframe to tell a better, more positive story. It's just a story, after all, and you can choose what you want that to be.

The young moms-to-be in my childbirth class were very close to their due dates and were eagerly awaiting their next set of hypnosis skills to help them through their physical and emotional marathons about to begin in a few short weeks. I had recently taught them about awareness and the ability to move out of the negative and into the positive to manage their mindset.

"I have something to tell you guys," Amanda said with excitement. "I had my specialist appointment this week, and when we got there, the specialist said he had some bad news. My baby is breech, and I'm going to have to have a C-section." Amanda's face fell as she recalled the news. "I totally broke down," she said, "I was a mess. All these terrible things were running through my mind. What if something goes wrong? What if I go into labor early? What if I don't heal right? What if I can't have a natural delivery next time? I just went on and on and on in my mind, and I was bawling. I'm sure the doctor thought I came a little unglued. I stopped, took a breath, and then, my awareness kicked in!" Amanda beamed. "My mind stopped, and I asked myself, WHERE AM I? I was clearly in the future negative, and it wasn't helpful. I was freaking out about stuff that hadn't happened. I shifted to the positive by telling myself all the amazing things about having a C-section. How great it would be because I got to choose the baby's birthdate. I could tell everyone to be ready for the call, no middle-of-the-night surprises! I would have a team of doctors scheduled and focused on the baby's safe delivery and my care. And I could get my hair and nails done and look amazing!" Amanda took a deep breath. "By the time I was done moving myself up into the positive, I was smiling and feeling so good! Of course, all this was inside my head, so I went from a complete mess to almost ecstatic pretty quickly. I do think the doctor thought I was a bit nuts."

Amanda lifted herself out of the negative spiral using her awareness (Where am I?) and then shifted and lifted herself into the positive by reframing the event. She told herself all the good things that would happen because of the change, and she did this all in about one or two minutes. She lifted her frequency to a positive place, leaving that doctor's office feeling excited and happy.

Two weeks later, Amanda went on to have a beautiful, healthy baby girl by scheduled C-section at the right time on the right day with the right people assisting. And she looked amazing too.

I tell this story often because it's a beautiful example of the power you have inside you to reframe to tell a better story and pull yourself up into a higher frequency of living, which makes everything around you . . . better.

Peeling away the layers to open yourself up to your own value and connect to radical self-love, your greater state of harmony and flow starts with awareness, mindset, and the upward journey of your frequency. Kathy used these tools as she started to move herself out of her complex and difficult negative spiral. She has moved along in the process toward her radical self-love and now lives in a hopeful place and feels good about her life and the choices she is making.

Are you ready to explore your awareness and mindset and move ahead with me into the joy and strength that radical self-love brings?

Look to your past for your mindset patterns. Set an intention to notice your mindset and the patterns as they happen in the moment. You can also use the programmable filter (RAS) tool to help you with awareness. The key is to notice where you are and then make the shift by reframing the thought or feeling. As you practice and get good at moving yourself, you will feel yourself elevate your frequency as you move to a better-feeling place.

Chapter 5

Hug Your Past and Let It Go

"Never let the past spoil your present or
govern your future."
– Unknown

"Was I meant to be broken?" Kim asked in our intake call. "My life has been one big ball of trauma, and I live in fear and terror every single day." Kim was sixty-four, confused, tired, and struggling. "I had such an awful family, no support at all, and my three sisters put so much hate onto me from an early age. I was emotionally abandoned. I remember the moment I abandoned myself. I gave up and became an empty shell. I was nine years old, and I stopped believing in myself or a future. At that point, I just gave up and turned it all inward on myself." Agoraphobic for a large part of her life, Kim also lived with chronic depression and anxiety. In this moment, she was completely blocked artistically, unable to sculpt. Sculpting, the one thing that brought her some peace and a sense of fulfillment, was no longer reachable.

After a recent stroke, Kim decided to find her way through the mess, back to herself, her purpose (her art), and learn how to love herself. The immense fear that had her in its grip her entire life was holding her in an ever-tightening embrace, choking off her life. She was scared.

When I met Kim, she had done a lot of work with doctors, counselors, acupuncturists, healers, and even a shaman or two. She was now officially desperate, which is where many of my clients are when they find me. "If I don't figure this out soon, this fear is going to kill me," she said.

A certain amount of fear is healthy. It's an autonomic response that is there to alert you when something may be wrong or if there's a perceived threat. It keeps you safe. Healthy fear helps you avoid dangerous situations or adjust your response to a situation or event. Unhealthy fear, as was the case with Kim, is fear that is running amok. It's out of control, making you more cautious than you need to be and preventing you from living your life.

Initially, Kim's fear was healthy and what you would expect in her trauma experiences, but as she became over-sensitized, the fear became unhealthy and overwhelmed her nervous system, and continuously dumped stress hormones into her body.

My first step with Kim? My mantra is always *trauma first.* I knew she needed to release the unresolved trauma to loosen the tight energy that was holding her hostage and to stop her physical nervous system response. In her current state, she was hypervigilant, fidgety, and completely unable to relax. This is a tough place to live your life, and Kim was certainly feeling it.

The trauma-release work with Kim was fast and powerful; she was ready for change. What Kim uncovered as a root source of this debilitating fear was the trauma of losing her twin in utero and the grief she carried with her from birth. When Kim released the trauma, what came to the surface for her was her innate strength and courage. This was her hug, the gift she took away from having gone through this. "He chose not to come," Kim said, referring to her twin, "but I persevered. So I guess I wanted to be here on some level even though it's been really rough." Kim could clearly see it, pick up the wisdom, learn from the experience, and then let it go.

The wisdom, learning, and acknowledgment for Kim were from a spiritual perspective that she **wanted** to be here. Understanding that ripped off a big layer of blockage for Kim and got her firmly moving toward her goal of loving herself. And sculpting again.

Like Kim, facing your fear in whatever form it takes is crucial to your success in reaching the golden destination of radical self-love, and starts your journey with a signal to the heart that says, "Hey, I'm on my way now. I'm worth it." Whether it's unresolved trauma, emotional blocks, beliefs that undermine you, or negative patterns you are looping in, peeling it off and letting it go (after the hug for all of the wisdom and learning, of course) is your way back to radical self-love. You are clearing the path to an open heart.

What's in the way of your open heart? Are you like Kim, a little constricted, emotionally blocked, or self-sabotaging? It took Kim a lot of years and mental and physical health issues before her awareness kicked in and showed her that love for herself mattered above all else and action was needed NOW.

What blocks your path, and are you ready to start clearing your way back to love? I can tell you that if you don't clear the way, the path grows smaller as the obstacles grow bigger. New obstacles get dropped in, and you will find yourself further and further away from radical self-love.

At the deepest yet simplest level, there are two states of being. There is the state of LOVE and all the emotions and feelings surrounding it: compassion, gratitude, grace, and joy. On the other side is the state of FEAR and all of fear's emotions and feelings, the traumas, anxiety, anger, hopelessness, and depression, to name a few. Your challenge? At any given moment, you can only be in one of these states operating and directing your life and experiences. You are either in LOVE or in FEAR.

Now you do fluctuate and move between love and fear, sometimes all day long. The big challenge is when you operate from the negative (fear-based) mindset rather than the positive (love-based) mindset, you are keeping yourself *down* in low frequency, AND in being in low frequency, you are separating yourself from the more significant part of you. And if you can't connect to that inner, beautiful part of you, you can't feel self-love.

Positive is your natural state; it is where your love lives.

Fear and the emotions and feelings fed by fear breed complication, chaos, and confusion. They keep you down, and in separating yourself from the true you and all the good feelings, guidance, and wisdom that lives there, you suffer. Your life suffers. People around you suffer. Maybe you live in drama, and maybe you live in anger. Maybe you live with anxiety or depression. The point is all these fear-based feelings create resistance inside you and to life and a tightness that keeps you from lifting into the higher frequency of love. Basically, you get stuck on the fourth floor.

All negative thoughts, feelings, and emotions are just fear, plain and simple.

This reinforces why the **awareness of your mindset and managing your mindset** is so important. Catching yourself to recognize you are in negative (fear-based) thoughts, emotions, and feelings is how you will change them and move back to the positive higher frequency place. And this is where radical self-love lives.

One of my clients was a very hard-working woman who started a coffee shop ten years ago and was having major challenges with the business now. It was hard to keep staff, and the business was losing a lot of money. Joan worked seven days a week, and truthfully, she wasn't letting staff do their jobs. So they left. Joan wanted to do some work around her fear-based beliefs about money, but what was really at play was a lack of self-love. At her core, Joan felt unworthy, and had built layer upon layer of fear blocks and limitations that kept her deep in her sense of unworthiness.

One of the fears that surfaced for Joan was about not being seen. "The business will fail if I'm not there" was her constant thought and was running her life. Joan had been adopted as a child and was raised by an unloving mother. She felt invisible and powerless in her childhood, and several events in her early life created a massive fear of not being seen. The block kept her stuck in *I need to be seen; I need to be there.* It was protecting Joan, but the impact on her life was that she *over-managed* and was working herself ragged. In understanding the purpose and the gift this fear was attempting to give Joan, she could let it go.

Joan did the work. She cleared out layers of fear and limitation and then rebuilt the connection back to her power and worthiness. She connected to radical self-love. She put herself first, not from a fear-based perspective but from a love-based perspective. She also sold the coffee shop and took on a different corporate job aligned with her re-established sense of self and self-worth.

Unresolved Trauma

We've all experienced some form of trauma. It's part of being human. Things happen to us. For some, it's small and manageable. For some, incredibly complex and a testament to resilience as to how these people have survived. For you, it may not have been a big dramatic event but a series of small, seemingly ordinary things that piled up and impacted your mind's ability to cope. For others like Kim, it may start with a dramatic life-changing event like the death of her twin, and then subsequent traumas pile up, making life heavy, dark, and grim.

In either case, if the traumas exceed your mind's natural ability to cope, you are left with emotions and physical responses that can overwhelm and sabotage your life. You are left with fear. Post-traumatic stress disorder (PTSD) occurs when the stress symptoms around the trauma persist, and you are repeatedly "triggered" back into those traumatic emotions and physical responses.

For one of my clients, Donna, a woman who was sexually assaulted in her teens forty years before coming to me, the effects of that event sat in the front of her mind and colored absolutely everything for her in the years that followed. The event and resulting fear were always "there" and became her lens through which she saw the world.

Looking at and healing trauma can be challenging and require courage and resolve. (*Note: You can choose to do this on your own. However, if this isn't comfortable or you are dealing with serious, complex trauma, PTSD, or mental health issues, please reach out and find assistance to help you through the process of resolving your trauma. Talk with a compassionate friend, a counselor, a hypnotherapist, or a healer to help you. You can find my contact information at the back of this book if you would like to work with me.*)

When you heal the trauma, you release its hold over your life. After doing trauma release work with Donna, she was amazed at how she felt and said with a smile, "It feels like it's FINALLY been put in the proper place. It's small and inconsequential." She pointed to the back of her head. "I can feel it in the back of my mind now, not the front. I feel so much lighter!"

The release of unresolved trauma takes you out of the cycle of stress, fear, and the heaviness and constriction it causes. As the dense and low vibration energy is removed, your frequency naturally lifts. New pathways to better and more joyful ways of living are opened up.

This is self-love in action.

Fear-Based Emotional Blocks

"The emotion of fear often works overtime." – Tara Brach

Artists get blocked, writers get blocked, and we all get blocked at one time or another. If you've felt blocked in some way, stuck, or like you just can't get past "that thing," you've experienced a fear-based emotional block. Blocks come in all sorts of shapes and sizes; over time, they can layer one upon another, gaining strength in keeping you put, like layering bricks. I've had emotional fear-based blocks that felt like a giant invisible, impenetrable wall right in front of me and blocks I felt in my body that were like an engaged emergency brake that didn't allow any movement. Whether they are in your energy field or your physical body, these wound-based blocks are being run by fear.

Blocks happen for a mass of reasons, and no two people will have the same block or set of blocks. They are as individual as you are. There is no "One size fits all." Your childhood and adolescence were ripe for the creation of blocks, which are based on the emotional wounds you experienced as you navigated the ups, downs, and experiential learning that molded you within the dynamics of your life.

As a child, it can be difficult to make sense of things, especially things that are harsh, traumatic, or unloving. Remember that the child you started as was connected to the loving self through your heart and expected love and nurturing. Through difficult experiences, that child's expectation dims. I'm not a neuroscientist, but I know that as a child, you are not working with a fully developed brain or the awareness to understand that the issues you lived with **were not your fault**. What you experienced likely has NOTHING at all to do with you and everything to do with the other person and their wounds and limited capabilities. Unfortunately, as a child with little emotional development and reasoning, you get wounded. When enough wounds happen, fear blocks are created, and they block you from feeling your goodness and self-love.

Childhood wasn't all that kind to Joan, and the result was many layers of fear built up in her body and energy that affected her ability to move. Like a deer in headlights, this block held her in *freeze* mode and created intense pain across her shoulders, becoming heavier and more debilitating as the years passed. Our work together revealed that this fear block was created when Joan was five. In trouble with her mom again, she was made to get the big spoon, pull down her pants and wait for her mom to come and spank her. She didn't even know what she'd done this time. The fear of her mom and being spanked lodged in her body in the shoulders, gut, and legs. It was a complete feeling of frustration, anger, and panic at being powerless and unloved. She described the block as being like a stick across her shoulders and knees and a round, simmering, hard mass in her gut that was black, dense, and heavy.

Joan connected to the heavy black "sticks" and discovered they were there to protect her. "It holds me together and wants me to be strong enough to leave," she said. "It wants me to know I am powerful, and this isn't my fault."

With the message received, Joan could slide out the sticks and release the black ball, transforming them into a butterfly that flew away. In the space, she added the white light of positivity and forgiveness.

With her learning and understanding in place, she now knew she didn't deserve this and that there was nothing wrong with her. Her shoulders and legs felt light, and her gut was loose again. She felt profoundly relieved and free.

How to Hug it and Let it Go

It may not seem like it in the moment, but everything you experience has the capacity to be a gift. Even the worst situations offer an opportunity to move to something better, whether it's something inside you, like a better attitude, understanding, or a new skill, or a better life situation, like a new job. Knee-deep in the difficult moments, though, it can be hard to see and appreciate this and to trust there is goodness to be had. When you can move beyond the emotion of the situation, the little (or big or *huge*) gifts will be waiting for you.

Move to Safety

When you are **IN** the fear, the vulnerability, the judgment, the anger, or whatever wound is activated in you, you must bring down the emotion to allow it to move through you and to bring safety to this moment. Once you are in safety and the difficult emotion has been moved, you can reach in for the learning.

Bilateral Stimulation

One of the best ways to bring down overwhelming emotion is through bilateral stimulation exercises. Bilateral stimulation uses body movement to *activate* or balance both sides or hemispheres of the brain, reducing the active, overwhelming emotion. It connects the emotional/feeling side of the brain, currently overloaded, and the thinking side of the brain and resets the nervous system. It's like pressing a giant reset button.

You can use it in two ways when you are actively IN the overwhelming fear or emotion to de-escalate it or to reprogram the *trigger* that takes you there.

In either case, you are interrupting the habituated pattern of emotion and rewiring your brain to a new response. After approximately three to six times consistent pattern interrupt (could be a little less, could be a little more), your brain will be rewired to move beyond the habituated response.

When I do trauma release work, I use a similar technique created by Nick Davies called BLAST (bilateral analysis and stimulation technique) for rapid release that uses patterns of eye movement to reprocess trauma across both hemispheres of the brain (see my website, www.elementalbalance.ca for more information on rapid trauma release using BLAST).

The whole process takes about one to two minutes. It involves moving some part of you (arms/eyes) back and forth across the midline of your body as you focus on breathing. This action forces both sides of the brain to engage (the reset) and *drains* any overactive energy happening in one hemisphere, effectively neutralizing the feeling. From there, you create the feeling you would rather have in its place using an affirmation.

1. Find an object that you can toss between your hands. This can be anything—a set of car keys, an orange, a hairbrush. It doesn't really matter what it is as long as you can catch it easily between your hands. If you don't have anything you can toss, or if you are a terrible catch, you can use your eyes.

2. Notice the moment the trigger/fear/anxiety begins. Focus on the feeling and give it a number between one and ten of the level of disturbance, where one is low, and ten is the absolute worst you've ever felt.

3. Focus on your breath. Gently toss the object from hand to hand, ensuring your hands swing out **across the midline (middle)** of your body and then back as you toss to the other side. If you aren't tossing anything and are using your eyes, look straight ahead so that your gaze is in the middle of the eye (not up and not down) and move your eyes from the outer corner of one eye to the outer corner of the other. Continue to focus on your breath as you toss or move your eyes.

4. Repeat for at least one minute or continue until you sense when the feeling "drops."

5. Stop tossing/eye movements, check in, and see where you are with the trigger/fear/anxiety and what number it's at now. Continue the process until it has completely dropped to zero.
   You have now interrupted the feeling/pattern, drained it out, and will create a new response.

6. From this place of calmness, think now about how you would like to feel.

7. Identify the positive feelings and the state you would like to be in. For example, if you were draining out *anger*, you might want to feel peaceful, calm, grounded, and confident.

8. Repeat mentally, "I feel [X]," or "I am [X]. I am calm. I am safe." As you think about each of those feelings and states, notice how they feel in your body. Really feel them as you bring them in and turn them up.

The beauty of bilateral stimulation is its effectiveness, and you can use it almost anywhere. In a grocery store lineup, toss your keys; while you are walking, swing your arms; or when you are doing just about anything, scan your eyes from left to right and back again.

My son was hit by a car as a pedestrian several years ago, and after he bounced off the car and fell to the pavement, the car sped away. No other cars or people were there, so as that car sped off, he was left lying in the middle of the road, completely unsupported. As you can imagine, this was a huge trauma for him, and he was lucky not to have sustained much physical damage. A week or two after the accident, when he was able to drive, he was triggered into extreme fear and anxiety when another car came too close to his. The roads are full of tailgaters, especially in the city, so it became a big problem. He was flooded with fear, anxiety took over, and then the anger would come. My son is a smart guy, and he knew this wasn't a good place to be and had no desire to end up being a road rager. Bilateral stimulation shifted all of this for him. When a car approached fast or came too close, he would turn on the windshield wipers and follow them with his eyes (bilateral stimulation) to drain out the fear and anxiety. Over a couple of weeks of consistently using his wipers, he completely rewired his brain and was confident and calm behind the wheel. The other good news was that the hit-and-run driver was caught and charged.

With emotions lowered, you are now ready to look at what you have gained from this situation. You will reframe the difficult or traumatic things as things that happened "to me" to things that happened "for me." This perception shift allows you to see and accept what you've gained by going through it. Ask yourself some of these self-inquiry questions for deeper understanding:

- **What is this fear/emotion/anxiety trying to teach me?**
- **What have I learned about myself?**
- **What strengths have I created that I take with me from this issue?**
- **What positive qualities do I have that have helped me through this?**
- **What is the biggest positive piece of learning I take away from having gone through this?**

New or stronger inner resources (perhaps strength, courage, resilience), positive qualities (like compassion, kindness, empathy), and wisdom (I'm never going to do that again!) will show themselves and become your gifts. And then you can let it go.

Somatic Imagery

Somatic means of the body, and this technique is exceedingly effective at removing fear blocks lodged in your energy field and affecting your body. You already know and are living the negative outcome of this block, so that isn't your focus with this technique. The goal here is to understand the block's positive intention and see what it's trying to help you with. When you pick up the learning and see the positive, you can change it or let it go completely.

1. Take a few deep breaths to get yourself into a relaxed state. You can do this with your eyes closed or open.

2. Check in with your body. Perhaps do a scan of your body and locate where you feel the fear or block.

3. Feel that block and identify the sensation. Is it hot, cold, tight, or tingly? Notice what it is for you.

4. Next, give that sensation a color and a shape.

5. Now, connect to this object, this color, and shape as though it had a consciousness, and ask what its positive intention is for you. How is it trying to help you, or what is it there to remind you of? Continue with this positive

inquiry and bring forward the positive message from this block.

6. Now ask yourself if you could change this object so it was more comfortable or was operating differently for you, OR if you could remove it altogether, what would you prefer?

7. If you are changing the object, allow that change to occur.

8. If you are removing the object, change it into something easy to remove, like a helium balloon and have it lift off, or a bird and have it fly away. After the object is gone, fill that space now with something positive, like light or flowers or whatever makes you feel good.

When you are done releasing the fear block, ask yourself these self-inquiry questions for deeper understanding:

- **What positive resources have I created for myself?**
- **How will my life be different now with this change?**

Bring down the emotion, mine the experience for the gifts, and then you can send the trauma and fear on its way.

In hugging your fear (and collecting your gifts), you've moved yourself closer to radical self-love. Radical self-love is fearless, and isn't that what you want? To be fearless and radiate out the love you have for yourself, in full expression to the world. Fearless. What would it be like to be fearless? What could you do in your life if you were fearless? How much love would you feel for yourself if you were fearless?

Your willingness to stop, look and heal those wounds and fears you've been carrying is an incredibly loving self-care practice that moves you closer to your own heart, your own value, and a place of deeper appreciation for yourself. You now know and understand yourself better. You've created space for positivity.

Know that when you take these actions to remove the darkness that dims your self-love, you put yourself in a better state of harmony and flow and, from there, a higher frequency of life. Your penthouse is getting closer.

Chapter 6

Un-Limit Yourself

"Perhaps the biggest tragedy of our lives is that freedom is possible, yet we can pass our years trapped in the same old patterns."
– Tara Brach

"I feel doomed," he said, "like I don't deserve friends or love." James, a young man in his early twenties, was suffering with depression, anxiety, and self-esteem issues. As a second-year university student, he struggled with acceptance, making social connections, and feeling overwhelming loneliness in his chest. James was soft-spoken and shy, never felt like he "fit," either in school or with his family, and he had been bullied throughout his high school years.

After a full session of trauma release, he moved through fear. The biggest was fear of abandonment and then betrayal, both triggered by two difficult romantic relationships and how each had ended not well.

"I have to try harder."

"There's something wrong with me."

"I mess things up."

"I'm always alone."

"I'm not fun."

These were some of the beliefs running below the surface that limited James and took him to a place where he could not feel good about who he was. Even deeper were core identity-limiting beliefs.

"I'm not good enough."

"I'm not lovable."

"I'm not worthy."

The limitations at his core identity level that were running were from an event that happened when he was very young. As a sensitive child, the meaning he made from this event created programming that told him he was a failure and worthless. Every issue, every slight, and every negative message after that reinforced these negative identity-level beliefs. The more it was repeated in his mind, the more evidence of it piled up, and the result was a deep depression, high anxiety, and extreme self-criticism.

James had been limiting himself at the identity level ("I am a failure, I am not good enough"), and you can't get much farther away from self-love than that.

He recognized the pattern in his two failed relationships of being "clingy" and putting himself down due to his low self-esteem. His belief in who he was (unlovable, unworthy) was feeding this pattern. Both partners had left because of the negativity and neediness, and it was just too much.

James brought these limiting programs to the surface, had the opportunity to understand what was supporting them, and then created and connected empowering beliefs.

"I am successful."

"I am confident."

"I am enough."

"I am wanted."

"I am loved."

"I am better than they think."

"I believe in me."

With his new beliefs in place, James stood taller and had more confidence. He discovered he liked himself and had much to offer this world. He started dating again, and now knowing his pattern of "clinging" and what was driving it, he was able to take a step back and focus on "I am enough" as a partner. James was moving himself to radical self-love.

When you stop and look at the programs running underneath the complicated feelings you have, the negative messages you tell yourself, the challenging situations you may be in, or the problematic social interactions you experience, you create an opportunity to see the whole picture and the patterns you may keep repeating. Beliefs that support and empower you give you the reach to step over those patterns and into radical self-love.

This theme is consistent with the people I work with—a struggle with personal worthiness and self-love. I hear their beliefs, "I don't deserve it, I don't matter, I'm not worth it." When these thoughts and feelings are active inside you, they become the underpinning of your life. This will be your home frequency, and everything around you will match it. Remember the mirror? Project out, "I don't deserve it, I don't matter, I'm not worth it," and this is what gets reflected to you in your life.

What do you believe about yourself and who you are? Do you believe you are magnificent and deserve everything in this world? Do you believe you are confident, amazing, and *worthy* of being here and living a big, huge heaping of prosperity and abundance? Would you like to?

To allow radical self-love in, you must go inside to understand how you have programmed yourself. To do that, you look at the messages and beliefs you accepted and created from the people around you and society. You look at the patterns in your life that hold you away from your best and make the decision right now to create positive unlimited programming that uplifts you and opens you to radical self-love.

A long time ago, a man went to see the circus. As he walked around the circus grounds, he saw many show animals in cages. He noticed several elephants standing together, unchained and uncaged. He was surprised to see that they were tied up by a thin, flimsy rope. These elephants were large, impressive animals, several tons each, and it was obvious they could easily break free of the rope, but they did not.

The man asked about the elephants and why they didn't break free of the flimsy ropes. The trainer told him that when they were young and much smaller, they used the same size rope to tether them, which was enough to hold them. As they grew up, they became conditioned to believe they couldn't break away. So they never try.

Because they believed they couldn't be free, they were stuck right where they were.

You have to identify your ropes, see how they limit you, and then "move your leg" to break free of them. Imagine how easy it would be for the elephant to just take one step forward and find itself unbound and free to choose where its next step would be.

When you came into a body as a newborn baby, you believed you deserved everything. You came in empowered. You believed you were magnificent and amazing and that the whole world was open to you. Through your experiences and the acceptance of the messages around you, you shifted out of that magnificence and created limited programming. Your programming affects everything in your life, money, love, how you feel about yourself, how you feel about possibilities, opportunities, the goodness in life, your purpose, and your path.

In Tony Robbins' book, *Awaken the Giant Within*, he states, "It's not the events in our lives that shape us, but our beliefs as to what those events mean." The meaning you attach and how you interpret that meaning will create either a life of joy or a life of despair. It will be a life connected to self and feeling love for yourself or a life disconnected and dark. He says that "global beliefs," the giant generalized beliefs you have about everything in your life (identity, people, work, time, money, love, and life itself), can shape and color every aspect of your being. That means "Making even one change in a limiting global belief can change virtually every aspect of your life in a moment."

That's good news!

What Is a Belief?

Esther Hicks of Abraham Hicks, an American inspirational speaker, channeler, author, and teacher of the law of attraction, says, "A belief is just a thought you keep thinking." Tony Robbins says, "A belief is a feeling of certainty about something." So if you have a thought, feel some certainty about it, and then keep repeating that thought (or see evidence of that thought in your life), you become more certain, right? And a belief is born.

Where do the thoughts come from that create beliefs?

Beliefs get created by you from external experiences or are given to you by others. Based on the messages you take in from others, especially in your childhood from your family and friends, you decide to notice, absorb, and accept that information which then easily becomes a belief or a system of beliefs. These come from school experiences, social situations, and the larger society. From that experience or message, you create meaning from it in relation to yourself.

Let's say, as a small child, you have the repeated experience of the kids in your class not picking you as a partner to line up with. You are the last to be chosen, often. The meaning you decide to take away from this is, "There's something wrong with me because I never get picked." You notice when the kids don't share with you, and that message is reinforced. "There's something wrong with me." You don't get a gold star on your workbook. "There's something wrong with me." Each situation reinforces the meaning you make, which creates the certainty that there *is something wrong* with you.

Remember the reticular activating system (RAS), the programmable filter the unconscious mind uses to bring something into your awareness? Each time you reinforce, "There's something wrong with me," the RAS brings you more. More reinforcement means a higher degree of certainty. That decision you made to accept "There is something wrong with me" is now a belief.

From your adult perspective, if you were to ask: Did these experiences mean something is wrong with me? Absolutely not. But to a six- or seven-year-old child attempting to make sense of their world, this is the meaning and the belief that becomes part of your programming.

Cultural conditioning is another way we create what is called **shared beliefs**. I was listening to the radio in my car on the way to an appointment and caught a fascinating super short story, a bit of a teaser for an upcoming show. A professor of sociology was talking about medieval times and how, way back then, the *left* side of anything was considered "bad." Seriously! Left-handers were considered to be possessed by demons. They were shunned, punished, or even worse, provided with torturous medieval "treatments" for their ailment (our poor lefties—they've definitely had a hard time of it over the centuries). The left sides of beds were pushed up against walls so one could only get out on "the right side of the bed." It's taken centuries to work this "Left is wicked" belief out of our cultural conditioning. You would think that this kind of societal belief that left-handedness was bad would have disappeared a lot sooner than in the 1940s or 1950s.

While it was tamed, it certainly wasn't gone when my nana was born in 1913. Unfortunately for her, she was born a left-hander. She endured a lot of "help" as the school and her family "retrained" her to write with her right hand because it was thought that left-handedness meant a deficit. My nana isn't with us anymore, but I wonder what identity-level beliefs she created from that experience.

Families give us beliefs as thoughts, concepts, and behaviors that are reinforced. Did you believe in Santa Claus when you were young or the tooth fairy? An authority told you it was true (you increase certainty because, generally, you trust your parents). Then with Santa, it was further reinforced once a year by society and culture, AND you probably got a cool gift from the guy. The tooth fairy story was further reinforced by the money under your pillow in exchange for a tiny white tooth.

The truth is the majority of your beliefs were created before you were seven years old. Think about that. You're letting a young child make lifelong decisions about who you are and what you're truly capable of. Another amazing fact is that all those decisions that created limiting beliefs were just someone else's opinion.

"I'm not smart" was the belief that Bonnie uncovered, created at the tender young age of nine. That particular year, she was uprooted and moved with her family to a brand new city, leaving her friends and extended family behind. It was a hard adjustment, and her school experience was tough on her. She had difficulty making friends, which created high stress, she couldn't concentrate, and her schoolwork suffered. Before that, Bonnie was typecast in the family as the "artsy" one and her brother as the "brainy" one. She was already poised and ready for a limiting belief about her intelligence, and this experience at nine tipped the scales.

"I'm not smart," ran her life. She felt like she was letting people down. She had to be better, and she had to be perfect. "Not good enough" bubbled up and created issues in her relationships. The funny thing was, even though Bonnie felt that she "wasn't good enough" and "wasn't smart," she graduated high school, went to university, and was a pharmacist running her own business. And still, the beliefs ran, and she continued to feel terrible about herself.

A core belief, like Bonnie's "I'm not good enough," is propped up by a cluster of supporting beliefs, such as her "I'm not smart," "I have to work harder," "I have to be perfect," and "I can't let people down."

Core beliefs are created in childhood and generally are at the identity level (**I am [insert your own words]**), and these continue to get reinforced throughout your life. The reinforcement is where your unconscious mind says, "Oh yes, I understand this; it's related to that message I took in back when you were four." And it gets deeper. And deeper. These core beliefs are so deep they are magnetized in your cells, and you begin to pull or magnetize situations (think frequency and law of attraction here), events, and people into your life that further reinforce the belief.

Changing Limiting Beliefs

Your programming based on beliefs will continue to run until you change them, either through awareness and with an intention to change or through enough changed *evidence* of that belief to shift it. All it took for Bonnie to remove "I'm not smart" from her program was to become aware of the belief and then fully see all the evidence of its falseness. As Bonnie discovered, the unconscious mind doesn't differentiate or consider the context when it's running something. Here she was, working against her own intelligence, just "getting through" school, as she put it, and yet graduating from university as a pharmacist and still feeling like she wasn't smart. Beliefs that are set up early on can continue to run and shape your life, EVEN IF it's detrimental to you. And, likely, you aren't even aware of it.

There are many ways to change beliefs, and many books have been written on how to do it. Regardless of the technique you use, the first step is to identify the belief that's running. **You must become aware of it** (awareness is the precursor to change).

You don't have to do a great deal of digging to see what beliefs are in your way. With intention and ten or fifteen minutes, you can bring to the surface the beliefs limiting you.

Identify Beliefs Exercise:

1. Have paper and pen handy and a quiet space to work in.

2. Set an intention to understand the limited beliefs creating the situation you want to change. For this exercise, focus on the beliefs that hold you back from self-love.

3. Get comfortable, close your eyes, and take three deep breaths to move yourself into relaxation.

4. You are going to move back in time now to a time when you were younger. For this exercise, you will return to being a teenager, then age eight, and finally age five. You can repeat this and take yourself back to any age when limited programming may have been created.

5. Take yourself back to when you were a teenager. Feel and experience yourself as a teenager.

6. Now allow all the people who gave you negative beliefs or negative messages about who they thought you were when you were a teenager to come forward. Hear what they had to say to you. Hear the messages they are giving you and notice the beliefs you are accepting. Let it happen rapidly, and have them continue to come forward until you have heard and seen them all.

7. Gently come up to the surface now and write down the messages and the negative beliefs you accepted as a teenager.

8. Close your eyes and take a deep breath in to relax again.

9. Take yourself back to when you were eight or nine. Feel and experience yourself as an eight or nine-year-old.

10. Now allow all the people who gave you negative beliefs or negative messages about who they thought you were at the age of eight or nine to come forward. Hear what

they had to say to you. Hear the messages they are giving you, and notice the beliefs you are accepting. Let it happen rapidly, and have them continue to come forward until you have heard and seen them all.

11. Gently come up to the surface now and write down the messages and the negative beliefs you accepted as an eight or nine-year-old.

12. Close your eyes and take a deep breath in and go back into relaxation.

13. Take yourself back to when you were five. Feel and experience yourself as a five-year-old.

14. Now allow all the people who gave you negative beliefs or negative messages about who they thought you were at the age of five to come forward. Hear what they had to say to you. Hear the messages they are giving you and notice the beliefs you are accepting. Let it happen rapidly, and have them continue to come forward until you have heard and seen them all.

15. Gently come up to the surface now and write down the messages and the negative beliefs you accepted as a five-year-old.

You can continue this process using any age that feels appropriate or directing yourself to go back to the messages and beliefs when you "lost your power" or "stopped loving yourself." Get creative!

16. Look at your responses at each age. What are the themes? Look at the negative messages and ask yourself, **"When I heard this message, what meaning did I make? What did I tell myself about myself?"** The goal here is to take the messages and identify the belief or beliefs that you created.

17. With these beliefs identified now, look at them across the ages. How are these related? Which of these are core beliefs at the identity level (they will begin with "I am [insert your belief]"), and which are related (supporting)?

Reprogram Limiting Beliefs

With your limiting beliefs identified, you can now move into a process of creating change, and there are several ways to do this. You can use one or all of these techniques.

1. **Collapse and rebuild the core belief.**

   Identify the core belief and the beliefs underneath it, supporting it, and propping it up. Tony Robbins calls this a tabletop, with the support beliefs being the "legs" of the belief. Take out the legs, and the belief collapses.

In the example of Bonnie, her core belief was "I'm not good enough," and the props or supports to that core belief were "I'm not smart . . . I have to do better . . . I have to be perfect . . . I let people down."

Look at each of the props and ask yourself, **"Is this true?"** For Bonnie, was it true she wasn't smart? No. And she had massive evidence to the contrary. That was one support gone. The next support, "I have to do better," wasn't true either. "I have to be perfect" was a no as well, and "I let people down" was definitely not true.

When you do this exercise, you will find the majority, if not all, of the supporting beliefs are NOT true from your adult vantage point.

If it feels like it might be true, dig into it. Ask yourself for the evidence (**"How do I know it's true?"**). And then ask for the evidence of it *not* being true (**"How is this not true?"**). Expand on the NOT true list to weigh the evidence and collapse the support.

With the supports gone, the core belief is weakened. Look at your core belief. In Bonnie's case, it was "I'm not good enough," and ask yourself, **"Is that true?"** It was a definite NO for Bonnie, and she was clear about that. Next, **identify what you would rather think and believe about yourself**. "I am enough," was Bonnie's new belief.

And now, with the new belief, create the supports that prop them up and identify the evidence that supports them. Bonnie's supports were "I am successful" (she had a degree, a profession, and had built a successful business). "I am powerful" (again, the evidence was her career, and she was well recognized and respected in her field). "I am capable" (she owned a home, did continuous education and personal growth education to keep improving herself, and was able to caretake elderly parents with love). "I am a good partner" (she was kind, generous, and loving to her partner of five years).

Now the game is to look for evidence in your daily life of the new core belief.

2. Tap in the new belief.

Look at your limiting core belief and ask yourself from your adult vantage point, **"Is that true?"** Look at that limiting core belief and tell yourself, **"That's not true because I am . . . ."** finishing the sentence to identify what you want to believe about yourself. **"That's not true because** (in Bonnie's case) **I am enough**."

With this new belief, **"I am enough,"** you are now going to *tap* it into your body and your energy field. Tapping or the Emotional Freedom Technique (EFT) has you tap on various points of your body to drain and change feelings. Using traditional Chinese medicine acupuncture points, you can "tap in" how you want to feel.

The point you will tap is on the triple warmer meridian, which is part of the heart and fire element. The triple warmer or triple burner, as it is sometimes called, is related to social relationships and how you show up in the world.

The point you will tap is on the back of your hand, between the baby finger and ring finger, just below the knuckle.

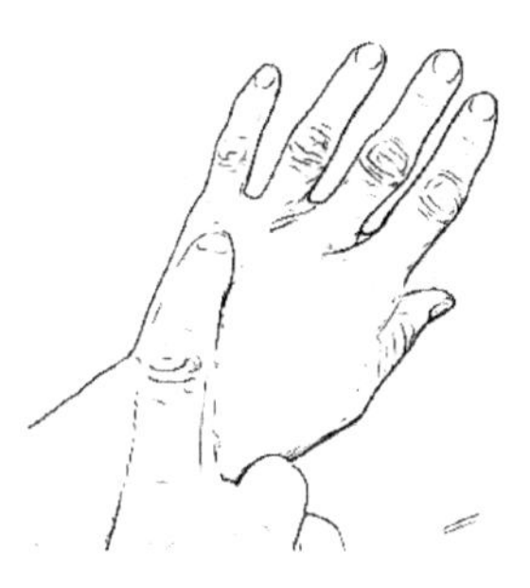

For this exercise, you will tap on the back of the right hand, but it doesn't matter which one you use. Take your left hand, and with three fingers, TAP that spot on the back of the right hand while you repeat your new belief out loud. Say it over and over again as you tap (in Bonnie's case, **"I am enough."**). You will do this for approximately one to two minutes. When you stop, take a moment and feel your expanded energy with this newly installed belief.

Tap daily for a week or two, once or twice a day, to anchor this belief.

Now the game is to look for evidence in your daily life of the new core belief.

3. Bridging.

Look at your limiting core belief and ask yourself from your adult vantage point, "**Is that true?**" Look at that limiting core belief and tell yourself, **"That's not true because I am . . . . ."** finishing the sentence to identify what you want to believe about yourself. **"That's not true because** (in Bonnie's case) **I am enough**."

This new belief will be the destination for your "bridge."

Imagine the old belief. Say it in your mind. And now, practice moving yourself to the new belief using a bridge of better-feeling thoughts and messages. The bridge you build could relate to the supports you have identified or can be positive phrases that move you to the new belief.

Using Bonnie's example, she would say, "I am not enough," or notice when this belief or message came up. She would immediately begin to bridge that thought/belief by saying something like this, "Hang on! There's that old belief, and that's not me. I know I am a good person. I am capable. I am kind. I am loving. I am powerful. I choose that **I am enough**."

She builds a bridge of more positive phrases that takes her to the new belief.

Strengthen New Beliefs

Once you have identified your new empowering beliefs, the reticular activating system (RAS) is a wonderful way to bring those beliefs into your awareness and show the unconscious mind that these are your new target. Create the RAS questions ("what" questions and "how will I" questions) to fine-tune and program the filter to anchor and bring the resources and evidence of your new beliefs into your experience. **"How will I feel I am enough today?" "How will I feel my worthiness today?" "How will I experience I am enough in my life and bring in all the goodness of that feeling today?"**

And then notice what shows up. See all the evidence of those new beliefs as you anchor them into your awareness.

Once you have your new belief and anchor it into your mind, you can play games with it. Look for evidence of the new belief in your everyday life. Use your new belief as your mantra as you fall asleep at night and as you wake up. Notice the supporting beliefs, too, and see the evidence of those. Get curious, get playful, and allow your awareness to show you how unlimited you are.

Negative Patterns

I was born in England in the sixties, and unfortunately for my mom, I was a breech birth. If you've never heard of that, it means the baby (me) doesn't turn itself properly in preparation for the birth, which is normally headfirst. Much to the huge delight and source of amusement for my siblings as we grew up, I was born "bum-first" because the doctors were unable to turn me into the right birthing position. Apparently, I was stubborn from the start. Of course, on a conscious level, I didn't remember my birth experience, but my mom sure did. In England, back in the early sixties, they didn't do C-sections often, so with no C-section and no drugs, she had me naturally, and it was a difficult and painful birth for her.

It's important to the story to know that I was wanted and deeply loved by both parents, and yet the way I came into the world created some deep issues for me that I was blind to for, well, decades. My birth was a traumatic event for my mom, and in my growing-up years, she would jokingly say to me, "You almost killed me!" This was always said with lightness, a wink, and a loving smile. However, to a young child, the meaning was clear: I was the cause of pain for my mom. I had done something wrong. Something bad happened, and I was at the center of it. This whole birth experience was lodged deep, and I know my mom would have been horrified to know how much those words affected me and how long I carried them.

I was a super sensitive child, and something deep inside me was affected by that birth experience. I always felt like I had to make things right with my mom. I needed to make her happy. When she would go to work, I would clean the house and vacuum to make sure she was happy when she came home (and I was young, probably eight or nine). I wasn't afraid. She never got mad. This was a profound feeling in me that I needed to "fix things" with my mom. My mom was a very happy person, and everybody loved her. I just had an internal driving need to make her happier.

The limiting belief of **"I have to fix this"** and **"I need to make my mom (and later "others") happy"** was created. As this limiting belief was reinforced, it became a pattern. My "people pleasing" negative pattern was born.

Although this negative pattern created good things in terms of accomplishments and being of service, it completely cut me off from exploring and understanding what **I** wanted for myself. It cut me off from **feeling** myself because everyone else came first. I was busy feeling for everyone else. This external need cut me off from my own self, my own self-love, and it was many years of people pleasing before I found my way back into balance.

Fear, energetic blocks, and limiting beliefs; there is an interplay between these that create patterns of behavior. We all have patterns running in our lives. We are creatures of habit and routine. Perhaps it's how you make decisions, the types of people you have in your life, or how you respond in situations.

I'm sure you know others (if not yourself) who bring the same type of people or the same difficult situations to themselves over and over and over again. When one toxic friendship ends, another one steps in to take its place. This is energetic patterns in action!

These unconsciously repeating patterns affect your sense of worthiness and how you see and accept yourself and can stop you from achieving the amazing things you came here to do. You may be overeating, not speaking up and retreating, or picking fights with your partners. Your traumas, fear blocks, and limiting beliefs feed into these patterns, which can affect EVERYTHING in your life: the choices you make, the partners you pick, the situations you allow yourself to be in, and how you manifest through your creative energy—or not.

My client was interested in understanding her negative pattern with men throughout her life, specifically with husbands! She had been married three times, divorced three times, and felt sick to her stomach at the thought of dating, yet she knew she wanted to be in a healthy, supportive relationship. It's what everyone wants, right?

Amrita was thirty-seven. She was from a traditional family from India and had one child, a son, from her third marriage.

Her first marriage was an arranged marriage at the age of sixteen. This situation created a great deal of resentment and anger in her toward her father, who arranged the marriage without her input. Unfortunately for Amrita, that's how things were done. That marriage to an older man lasted four years, and she was divorced at the age of nineteen.

Amrita married a second time at twenty-two to a man she'd known for a matter of weeks. In essence, it was like the arranged marriage because there was no courtship and no understanding of what marriage meant to either of them. This marriage lasted less than a year.

Amrita dated over the next few years and focused on healing the relationship with her father. When she was twenty-seven, she met her third husband through her brother. They got to know each other for six months before tying the knot. This marriage lasted eight years, and they had a son before divorcing.

The fear, beliefs, and patterns Amrita was experiencing were undermining her ability to find and keep a healthy love.

That sick, nauseating feeling was fear stuck deep in her stomach created in her second marriage. The fear's intention was to remind her that "She allowed it" and to show her she needed to "Stand up for what you want."

The belief she created from her sixteen-year-old arranged marriage experience was, "I am powerless," supported by "I have no control," "I can't have what I want," and "My voice doesn't matter."

This system of beliefs that reinforced her lack of personal power when it came to choosing love and navigating relationships had her bump into two subsequent marriages that each had aspects of the arranged marriage—little to no love, unfulfilling, and ending in divorce. When she dug into understanding what the pattern was showing her, the response was, "Marriage without love, real love." The big aha for Amrita was the next step. **What was she to learn from this pattern**? The message was she needed to "understand what real love was, and that had to start with loving herself."

At the end of our work together, Amrita was clear she was to explore everything she had a love and passion for and to put herself first. She would work on what SHE wanted, what was important to her, and to love herself first. The rest would follow.

Breaking a Negative Pattern

The key to breaking a negative pattern is awareness. There it is again, the power of awareness! When you can identify a pattern, then you can transcend it. Awareness is always the precursor to change. There is learning in every pattern we uncover, and so like fear, you must understand the learning before it will fully let go. In fact, the pattern will keep repeating until you get the WHOLE lesson from it.

The timing of awareness with patterns can be interesting. You might become aware of the pattern the first time **after** the situation or event is over. That friend that was toxic. Maybe you recognize the pattern of the toxic friend after the third or fourth one leaves your life, although I hope you figure it out sooner. Whenever it is, it's perfect because **anytime awareness shows up, it means you are ready for change.**

So you find a new friend, thinking this will be different, and it's going really well, at least in the beginning. A little time passes, and you start to notice some of the same toxic behaviors creeping in. This is perfect too! You are now ***in*** **the pattern** when you notice it. Brilliant! Awareness is moving you along.

That friend leaves, and before you know it, you are faced with another new person stepping in. This time, awareness kicks in ***before*** the friendship begins, at the ***start*** of the pattern. All the warning signals are there that this could be the making of another toxic friendship.

To change the pattern, ask these questions:

1) **"What am I supposed to learn from this pattern**?" Really listen to the answer. In this example, you may understand that you need to "Be discerning, find people who have the same value of kindness as you, and put yourself first."

2) **"What can I do differently to change my response to this pattern?"** Stop and listen, and allow the answer in. For this example, the answer might be to "Politely decline the invitation and move on."

Negative patterns limit you and keep you from moving forward in your life. Until you gather up **all the learning** from the pattern, it will keep repeating. If you notice a pattern comes back, all the learning (or new learning) needs to be mined. Dig deeper, pull up the lesson, and then let it go. This will allow you to lift yourself up into a higher frequency of life and get closer to radical self-love.

What limiting beliefs and negative patterns are running in your life? What do you need to learn from these limitations? Can you identify the areas in your life where changes need to be made? Is it changes to who you think you are, people, work, time, money, love, or life itself? To feel love for yourself and be in a radical self-love state, you must become aware of the limitations driving your thoughts, behaviors, and patterns and **then change**

them. Only then will you open your heart and expand your potential to elevate your life.

Making these changes isn't hard and doesn't take a lot of great digging. Start from where you are and fine-tune your awareness to include your beliefs and patterns and how you may be limiting your potential. If you follow these steps and become aware of how you are moving through life, you can adjust into a better way, a way that takes you into deep love and appreciation for yourself and your life. A compassionate way. When you make these positive changes inside yourself, everything around you changes for the better too. Life unfolds in beautiful ways.

Chapter 7

Make Friends with Your Emotions

"Our feelings are our most genuine paths to knowledge."
– Audre Lorde

"I'm so ANGRY with her," Cliff said. "All I have to do is imagine her face or say her name, and there it is, up it comes, and I just want to pop her one." His face grimaced, and his body went rigid as his arm swung out as if he were landing a punch. Cliff was angry, and every fiber of his being was radiating it. "I don't know how I was married to that woman for so long," he said. "She's impossible to get along with and has to control every single thing." He took a deep breath and relaxed back into the chair. Cliff was in my office; his ex-wife was hundreds of miles away in another city, and yet she still had the power to completely derail Cliff and send him into an anger-fueled orbit.

Four years ago, at sixty, he remarried, this time to his "soulmate." A few months ago, he and his new wife moved to a new city for a fresh start. Cliff had no children; however, he and his ex-wife shared his beloved cat, and the plan was that Cliff would take the cat back once he was settled—in a month or two. Like it or not, his ex-wife was in his life a little longer.

Cliff's health had suffered on and off throughout his life, with two heart attacks, and two separate cancers.

In our work together, Cliff engaged with the anger and came to understand that the anger wanted him to stand up for himself. He had difficulty speaking up and was completely bowled over and shut down when his ex-wife would get "bossy," demanding and controlling how things would go and how he "should" be feeling and reacting. He needed a clear boundary to take back his power, and without it, the anger grew. And grew.

Cliff released fears that stemmed from his childhood and examined and changed his limiting beliefs about speaking up into empowering beliefs that supported expressing himself ("I am safe to use my voice"). He used the reticular activating system technique to become aware of situations and his own power in speaking up. It helped him be aware, practice daily, and see his good results.

Feeling more assertive, he decided he would stand up for himself and created "ground rules" (boundaries) for communications with his ex-wife. As anger came up, he would become aware and shift out of the old pattern that he slipped into and into his new pattern of self-honoring and boundaries.

The anger got smaller and smaller, and then quite quickly, it was no longer the main attraction in the relationship with his ex-wife.

Cliff used anger as a cue to speak up, and in doing that, he built the confidence to put himself first.

The main point here with Cliff wasn't the anger or boundaries, which are important, but the way in which he used his negative, overwhelming emotion as his cue to make a change. Any negative emotion is there to tell you something. It's telling you that you are cut off from who you really are, from your heart. And it doesn't feel good.

When you can become aware of what a negative or difficult emotion is showing you and see how you are cutting yourself off, you can interrupt it and make a choice to shift into something better for yourself. The anger in Cliff showed him he was miles away from his true state (love). The bigger the negative emotion, the farther away you are. Inquiry into the emotion will give you the key (Cliff's key: "Stand up for yourself") to return back to the true you.

What is your emotional messenger trying to tell you?

Check in with your default negative emotions. Are they small, once-in-a-while things? Or are they the huge "I'm living here full-time" ones? In either case, when you reflect on them, think about the situation, the triggers, and then the learning. As you reflect on that moment of negative emotion, notice how far away you were from your true self and self-love.

Suppressed Emotions

I spent a lot of my life not feeling. From a very young age, the world was overwhelming, and since I was a highly sensitive kid, it was often just too much. I was raised in the era when feelings weren't usually acknowledged, especially negative ones. "Say you're sorry" is what the three of us were told when sibling fights broke out. In that short-term win for the adults (no blame here—three kids is hard work!), there was no conflict resolution or learning to manage big emotions.

Where do they go? They get buried, pushed down, and suppressed. For years this worked well for me. If I didn't feel or acknowledge them, they would just go away. I could be busier and do more if I wasn't dealing with difficult feelings. And that was true, for a time anyway.

What goes in must come out, right? Suppressed emotions will eventually bubble up to the surface and let you know they are there at some point, having a significant effect on your emotional experiences. If you are cut off from yourself like I was, like my mom was, and her mom before her, it may show up as a thread of anger bubbling below the surface of everything in your life. Even though you smile and laugh, you don't fully feel it because the anger tamps it down. The bigger issue when you suppress emotions is that you cut yourself off from ALL emotions, even the great ones. You can feel them, but they are dulled.

If you don't allow yourself to feel, how can you feel love for yourself?

An article in *Medical Anthropology Quarterly* (Vol 8, No. 4) discusses a term North Brazilian women use called "swallowing frogs" to describe suppressing negative emotions: hatred, anger, jealousy, fear, irritation, and putting up with being treated badly in silence. The article goes on to say that these "frogs" would then create sickness in both mind and body. The theory behind the folklore was that the strong negative emotions that were "swallowed" (anger, anxiety, envy, fear) created social, physical, and emotional harm.

This pressure cooker of emotions can make you less resilient and more aggressive (short fuse!), and the increased stress on the body through the continual effort it takes to keep the emotions at bay takes its toll on your nervous system, your cardiovascular system, increases cancer risks and can lead to early death. Think about Cliff, with his short fuse and a lifetime of major medical issues relating to heart health and cancer.

Swallowing frogs is not an act of self-love.

Suppressed emotions must go somewhere. They will go deep into the body and create illnesses and/or will bubble up and overwhelm your life. My nana, whom I loved very much, was what my mom called "a volcano." She would suppress her emotions, stay silent, build up resentment, then the tiniest provocation and no warning, BAM! she would explode. Her body couldn't hold anymore, and up it came in all its glory. All those suppressed emotions would be strewn all over whoever happened to be lucky enough to be with her (usually my mom, who was an only child).

Do you remember the story of Pandora's Box? The Greek God Zeus gave a box to Pandora and told her never to open it. Pandora couldn't contain her curiosity, and against his instruction, she opened the box, releasing all the miseries that humans endure: greed, envy, hatred, pain, hunger, poverty, war, and death. Pandora tried to shut the lid, but it was too late. Underneath all those miseries was the thing that remained inside the box—**hope**.

If you think of any suppressed emotions inside you as your Pandora's Box, curiosity will be your key to opening that box and letting the long-suffering emotion rise up and leave you. It may not be comfortable; it may not be clean. It will be where your hope is, and that will lead you to joy.

After my divorce, I knew I had to do something to get that anger and suppressed emotion up and out of my body after years of living my disconnected (but very productive) life. I had a lot to clean out. I had just watched my mom go through two rounds of breast cancer, survive a debilitating stroke, and then succumb to an early death. I knew her lifetime of swallowing frogs led to her physical decline. I also knew that wasn't going to be me.

One of my dear friends recommended a weekend retreat that she had gone on years before to free the heart, so I eagerly signed up. I was ready. Over the weekend, the group spent thirty hours together releasing old emotions through breathwork, sound (loud sound), and focused exercises to pull up and move the emotion through the body.

One of the exercises was quite colorful, literally. First, we thought of the situation or person that brought up the emotion that needed to be released. Once there and once "in it," we blew up a balloon. We imagined we were blowing emotion into the balloon. Then we tied off the balloon and used a felt pen to write the person's name and/or the situation and emotion on the outside of the balloon. And we kept going. After about thirty minutes, the room was completely filled with colorful balloons. We did a deep healing meditation, and then the fun part: We popped our balloons which was a powerful physical action in the body.

Sound like screaming and wailing is another way that emotion can be released from the body. Now I'm not saying you should open up and start screaming (you'll scare your family or your neighbors), but I do know from my own experience and the past life regression work I do that the creation of a focused deep internal sound to express the emotion, like screaming, wailing, or even just blowing as you make a sound will move the emotional energy out.

I've never dug so deep and let go of so much. Letting go of the years of emotion stuffed down created space for me to get to know my emotions and engage with them in the way we all were meant to. It allowed me to feel again, especially the incredible high-frequency emotions like compassion, gratitude, joy, and self-love.

Many of us can stop and look at our emotions and work with them to pick up the messages and use the techniques outlined here to release them. **If it feels too big for you**, if you are dealing with serious, complex trauma, PTSD, or mental health issues, please reach out and find assistance to help you through the process of emotional clearing. Talk with a counselor and find a good hypnotherapist, a sound, breathwork, or energy healer to help you. (You can find my contact information at the back of this book if you would like to work with me.) **Be compassionate with yourself**. Trust, listen, and love yourself enough to reach out if you need something more.

Emotional Guidance

Your emotions are your guidance system. Simply put, you are being guided to do more of the things that create happy, uplifted, positive emotions and less (or none) of the things that create unhappy, downer negative emotions. Positive emotions are where you find your true self. Your guidance system is trying to show you in that moment of anger, jealousy, and hatred that the feeling you are in is far away from your true state of love.

Not all is lost. You can use those unhappy, downer emotions to find your way back. They help you to understand in what ways you are cutting yourself off so that you can stop, learn, and adjust into a better feeling emotion. Let's say you have a friend that frequently "forgets" to bring their wallet out for coffee. Each time you cover their double-whip mochaccino without standing up for yourself, you get a little more resentful. By the tenth time (if the friendship lasts that long), you are fuming. You don't even want to GO for coffee. What is your guidance system telling you? TAKE ACTION. Say something. Stand up for yourself. Get a better friend.

In his book *Awaken the Giant Within*, Tony Robbins talks about your emotions being a **signal to action**. That's a guidance system—take action. He goes on to say, "You can't avoid feeling, so learn to find the hidden, positive meaning in those things you once thought were negative emotions" and "If the message your emotions are trying to deliver is ignored, the emotions simply increase their amperage; they intensify until you finally pay attention." You must understand the message, so get curious. Become friends with your emotions.

One particular emotion coaching program I studied defined four main emotions and their unique response needs. These were:

1) **Shame** – needing reassurance.

2) **Sadness** – needing comfort or soothing.

3) **Anger** – needing support to create or assert a boundary.

4) **Fear** – needing safety or protection.

Tony Robbins takes this concept further in his book and lists ten of the (negative) "take action" emotions and what he feels those action signals are needing. Ultimately, you will discover what your emotions need and the direction they are giving you in order to return to that better state of love and connection to yourself.

Not only are your emotions your guidance system, but they are also key to raising your frequency.

All emotions have a frequency. Can't you just feel it when you are with someone who is depressed or angry? The low vibration just oozes off them, and it's uncomfortable. You can also feel the high vibration or frequency of someone who is in love, compassionate, or filled with gratitude. They feel amazing to be with. When you experience emotion, it affects your "home frequency." When in a negative emotion or stuck in an unhealthy emotion or suppressing negative emotion, you are lowering your vibration. And the mirror of your life reflects that lower frequency back at you.

It's worth repeating: **Positive is your natural state. It is where your love lives.**

Make friends with your emotions and use them as they were intended, as your guidance system. This means you are now navigating your responses and life and can move yourself up to a higher (more vibrant) frequency of living.

Esther Hicks and "Abraham" (an entity or group consciousness from the nonphysical dimension she channels, hits this point home with Abraham and Esther's scale of emotions/feelings, rated from highest to lowest vibration. Your aim, of course, is to be in the number one spot at Joy / Knowledge / Empowerment / Freedom / Love / Appreciation.

If you find yourself somewhere lower, your task is to move yourself up the scale toward a better feeling emotion. Each level-up moves you into a better feeling emotion and a high-frequency vibration.

Looking at the scale of twenty commonly felt emotions, you can easily see that to be in unworthiness, powerlessness, and insecurity is the lowest vibration you can be in. Lack of self-love *is* unworthiness *and* powerlessness. If radical self-love lives in the number one spot, you've got a hefty gap to close.

Understanding where you are on the scale requires awareness. The practice of mindfulness, being aware in the moment, will allow you to observe that emotion and let it pass, and then reach for a better feeling, thought, or emotion. As you notice, then clear, you lift into a better feeling place.

Take a moment and review the list. Where would you be? Are you stuck at one level, or do you cycle up and down the scale on any given day? Where does your default emotion sit? And most of all, how big is the gap between where you are and the number one spot?

1. Joy / Knowledge / Empowerment / Freedom / Love / Appreciation
2. Passion
3. Enthusiasm / Eagerness / Happiness
4. Positive Expectation/Belief
5. Optimism
6. Hopefulness
7. Contentment

8. Boredom
9. Pessimism
10. Frustration / Irritation / Impatience
11. Overwhelm
12. Disappointment
13. Doubt
14. Worry
15. Blame
16. Discouragement
17. Anger
18. Revenge
19. Hatred/Rage
20. Jealousy
21. Unworthiness / Insecurity / Guilt
22. Fear / Grief / Depression / Powerlessness / Victim

A Special Note on Forgiveness

Forgiveness is not on the list of emotions, but it does hold a special place in the quest for radical self-love, as it greatly impacts how you move up or down the scale. The situations that have created the lower-level emotions—the fear, pain, and wounds—hold us back from moving up to joy, love, and empowerment. To return to the lightness of loving yourself, these heavier emotions, feelings, and frequencies must be let go of.

Like a cork that bobs in the water, you naturally gravitate and are pulled UP to the surface. The lower-level emotions are heavier and hold you down under the water. True forgiveness dissolves the fears, hurts, and pains, and from there, you bob up to the surface and become closer to your natural state of love. You open yourself toward greater feelings of appreciation, worthiness, and radical self-love.

"Regardless of whether or not he deserved my forgiveness, I deserved peace." Thordis Alva describes in her TED talk "Our Story of Rape and Reconciliation" with Tom Stranger her rape at sixteen (by him) that led to eight years of reconciliation and forgiveness. She went on to say that forgiveness was her self-preservation.

Forgiveness is for YOU. You are the one that carries the heaviness, and so forgiveness is about lightening YOUR load, not someone else's. While forgiving someone else may allow them to let go of a piece of their heavy load (and then work on forgiving themselves), the act of forgiveness is about YOU casting off the heaviness so that you can "pull up to the surface" and live in a lighter way.

Forgiveness for yourself is an integral part of the forgiveness process, as often, we are hardest on ourselves. Sitting in self-judgment—another form of self-criticism—separates and holds you away from self-love. Be compassionate with yourself, and know that when you can turn your forgiveness inward, you are loving and accepting yourself.

What areas of forgiveness need exploring in your life? How can you offer yourself forgiveness?

Moving Emotions with Mindfulness

There's a lot of buzz out there about the mindfulness movement and being in a mindful state. Just what does that mean?

Mindfulness as a way of being is having your mind in the present moment and being aware of what's happening right NOW. It's the opposite of being out in the "future" or rushing around doing too many things at once. Mindfulness means you slow down, take your time, and be **aware** of the moment you are in.

Often confused with meditation, mindfulness can be a form of meditation and/or a daily practice and way of living. When you are mindful, you practice **observing with awareness** in the moment, which slows down the mind. You do this with "nonreactivity" or nonjudgment and with a hefty, healthy dose of self-compassion.

Mindfulness was created about fifty years ago in the Western world, which means it's a Western version of meditation. It was created for the purpose of living life in today's fast-paced world so that you experience less stress and anxiety, feel more peaceful, and deal with pains and illnesses, both psychological and physical. Mindfulness is calming and grounding and provides you the opportunity to decide how you want to react.

Your mind is conditioned to react. Whatever it approaches, it immediately judges and produces a series of thoughts and emotions or internal reactions to whatever is happening. By now, you have a clear idea of what you like and don't like, what you expect and don't expect, and what you need and don't need, creating a clear list of reactions to the moment. This is the foundation from which you judge your reality and your environment. Whatever those reactions are, they are not random. There is a pattern to your reactions that comes from your programming, including negative reactions to difficult emotions.

There are two ways we usually approach difficult emotions. The first is to **suppress or avoid or deny the emotion**, push it away, or stuff it down. Let's say you have an uncomfortable feeling; something is coming up. You might turn on the television, call a friend and go out, or check your social media—anything to move your attention somewhere else. Then you don't have to feel what's going on inside because it's uncomfortable. That feeling doesn't go away, it just grows inside, but still, you can short-term avoid what's moving within you.

The second way is to get **stuck in the emotion**. You might stay at home, cry a lot, and think a lot about who said what to whom, and why, and where, and how. It's as though the emotion takes over. You don't have the capacity to observe it or sit still with it. It triggers a lot of reactions, and you're lost in it.

In both approaches, you are having a **reactive relationship** with the emotion. And what reaction does is create the **growth of the original emotion**. It makes it grow, and it imprints the emotion deeper within you.

Dr. Itai Ivtzan, positive psychologist and professor at Naropa University and an incredible meditation and mindfulness teacher, remarked in a video, "Imagine your emotion is a bonfire. There's a fire in front of you, and it's burning. It's the fire of your sadness, your anger, or jealousy. Every time you react to it, you add wood to the fire. Try to push it away? You've added wood to the fire. You're in the drama—who said what to whom—and you are adding wood to the fire. Anything you do with the emotion in response to the emotion, it's wood to the fire, blazing, growing bigger and hotter."

There is a third way to approach difficult emotions: through mindfulness and being **non-reactive**.

Now, imagine you are at that bonfire, and you see the fire in front of you. This time, allow yourself to feel the emotion, to feel the sensations and emotional triggers inside you, but with **no reaction to any of it**. You sit still, and you observe the emotion and sensations that are triggered. That's it. You breathe into the sensations, into the emotion. This is the entire experience with whatever wave of emotion is moving, whatever the emotion, sensation, and internal experience is.

Compassion is very important here because some of these waves may be deeply painful. You don't have to throw yourself deeply into that wave and just stay there no matter how painful it is. That's not the case. Be compassionate and allow yourself to observe **as much as you can tolerate**. When it feels too much, take a step back and then engage with it when you're able and ready, and then take a step back when it's too much. This is a **healthy relationship** with emotion. Self-compassion and caring are very important aspects of this practice.

When you are able to observe the emotion and the sensation without reaction, the emotion dissolves.

The emotion dissolves because there is no more wood on the fire, no reaction, and nothing to feed on. **The emotion has been feeding on your cognitive and emotional reactions.** When there's no reaction, it gradually disappears, and you've let go of it.

As a meditation and mindfulness teacher, I use both meditation and mindfulness every day to manage emotions, reduce stress, and generally just get way more out of life. It's allowed me to process suppressed emotions and manage my daily emotional experiences in the moment as I deal with other people, difficult situations, and stress. Through mindfulness practices, I know myself better, feel better, and am more connected to my body.

When you practice mindfulness, you are no longer being bumped around in life, in "reactivity" mode. Nonreactivity and nonjudgment allow you to be okay with whatever emotions are present, which puts you back in the driver's seat of your life. That driver's seat gives you the gift of choice and a deeper connection to yourself. From there, radical self-love grows, and your vibrant life is expanding.

Get Friendly and Let Them Go

The first step in understanding and freeing your emotions is awareness. You must become aware of your emotions (or lack of emotions) so that you can befriend them, use them as your guidance system, and then let them go. You must recognize you are having an emotion when the emotion rises and then **interrupt that emotion** to understand what it wants for you. If you are suppressing emotion, you must recognize and interrupt that pattern of avoidance or distancing.

A great resource to understand your relationship with your emotions is to look at your past. Pick out several difficult situations you've been through and ask yourself these questions:

- **What emotion was present?**
- **What did I do with that emotion? Did I distance myself or avoid it? Did I get stuck in it?**
- **What is my pattern with difficult emotions?**

If you need to develop awareness in the moment, you can do this with intention. Set your intention to be more present with your emotions, either at the start of your day or before you go into situations that you know may bring up an emotion or two. And then watch for it.

Self-compassion and acceptance are critical parts of this journey. Through all your emotional inquiry, be kind and suspend judgment of yourself—practice self-forgiveness. Also, be kind to the emotion, acknowledge and appreciate it, and thank it for showing up as a resource **here to help you**.

The second step in understanding and freeing your emotion is once you've noticed the emotion, interrupt the pattern of expressing or suppressing it by asking one or all of these questions:

- **What is this emotion wanting to tell me?**
- **What does this emotion want me to do to help myself?**
- **What do I need to learn from this emotion?**

When you have uncovered the guidance from the emotion, it will begin to dissipate. Acknowledge and appreciate the emotion for being **here to help you.**

If you need to, you can use one of the following techniques to help you move into a better-feeling emotion.

1. Bridge to a Better Emotion

Look at the emotion present, and after you have your guidance, ask yourself, "**How do I want to feel**?" Once you have that new emotional target, you can bridge yourself to it.

The better-feeling emotion will be the destination for your bridge.

Now move yourself to the new emotional target by building a bridge of better-feeling thoughts and messages. In the example of Cliff, he was in anger and got the message to stand up for himself. That would feel **empowered** (his new emotional target). Now he can either remember a time when he felt like that or if he didn't have an example, he can imagine how it would feel to be in an empowered state. He would stand taller, and he would smile. He would feel confident, expanded, and powerful. By describing the emotional state he wants to be in, he takes himself there.

2. Get Your Body Moving

Emotion follows motion, so get your body moving to change your emotional state. Go for a walk, or if you can't do that, do some stretching, maybe a few yoga poses, or jumping jacks. Dance, move to some invigorating music. Get your body moving and shift out of the old emotion and into a new, better feeling.

3. Tap in the New Emotion

As with beliefs, you can tap in how you want to feel (your emotional target). Ask yourself, **"How do I want to feel?"** In the case of Cliff, he wanted to feel empowered.

With this new emotional target, **"I feel empowered,"** you are now going to tap it into your body and your energy field. Tapping, or the Emotional Freedom Technique (EFT), has you tap on various points of your body to drain and change feelings. Using traditional Chinese medicine acupuncture points, you can tap in how you want to feel.

Make sure your emotional target is the present and in the positive.

It's not:

"I *don't want* to feel [emotion]."

Or

"I *want* to feel happy."

Your present, positive target would be this instead:

"I am feeling happy."

Or

"I am happy, feeling abundant, and grateful."

The point you will tap is on the triple warmer meridian, which is part of the heart and fire element. The triple warmer, or triple burner as it is sometimes called, is related to social relationships and how you show up in the world.

The point is on the back of your hand, between the baby finger and ring finger, just below the knuckle.

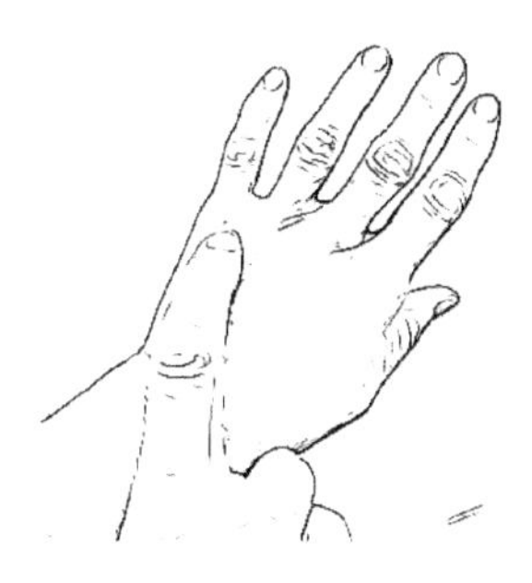

For this exercise, you will be tapping on the back of the right hand, but it really doesn't matter which one you use. Take your left hand, and with three fingers, tap that spot on the back of the right hand while you repeat your emotional target phrase out loud. Say it repeatedly as you tap. You will do this for approximately one to two minutes. When you stop, take a moment, and feel your expanded energy and connection to how you wanted to feel (In this case, Cliff felt empowered).

4. Sound Toning

Toning uses your human voice to release and heal. The process allows sound to move through you, playing you like an instrument, aligning frequencies, clearing, opening, removing blockages, and aligning all cells to a core vibration.

1) Locate the part of your body where you feel the emotion.
2) Stand and breathe in deeply. Expand your lower stomach as you inhale. Imagine the energy of each breath coming into your body through the area of the emotion. Choose the tone from the list below that corresponds to the area of the body where the emotion is felt. Use the exhale to make the tone as long as you can.
3) Repeat seven times.

- **Feet, Tone "UUUUUH"** – From the base of the spine down to your feet (root chakra energy center). Make an "UUUUUH" sound, as in the word ***cup***, a low guttural sound gently riding on the breath.

- **Lower Back, Tone "EEEWWW"** – From the belly button down to the base of the spine (sacral chakra energy center). Make an "EEEWWW" sound, as in the word ***you***, slightly higher pitch but still low.

- **Stomach, Tone "OHHHH"** – Just above the navel up to the bottom of the rib cage (solar plexus chakra energy center). Make an "OHHHH" sound, as in the word ***go***, slightly higher pitch.

- **Chest Area, Tone "AAHHH"** – At the center of the chest, at the heart level (heart chakra energy center). Make an "AAHHH" sound, as in the word ***ma***, higher pitch.

- **Throat Area, Tone "EYE"** – At the throat area (throat chakra energy center). Make an "EYE" sound, as in the word ***my***, high pitch.

- **Forehead, Tone "AYE"** – At the forehead (third eye chakra energy center). Make an "AYE" sound, as in the word ***say***, high pitch.

- **Head, Tone "EEEEE"** – At the top of the head (crown chakra energy center). Make an "EEEEE" sound, as in the word ***me***, high pitch.

When you've finished toning, stand and notice how your body feels in the area that was previously filled with negative emotion.

You can tone *all* the areas in your body as a daily practice to invigorate and clear your body. Do these in the order listed above, repeating each tone three times before moving to the next. Toning will help you to be energetically clear and heal internally with sound. Doing this will elevate your vibration and frequency.

5. **Use a Mindfulness Practice**

- Sit comfortably and focus on your breath as it moves in and out of your body.
- With compassion and acceptance, notice where you feel the emotion in your body. Notice the sensation.
- Focus your breath on this area of your body. Imagine you are breathing in and out of this part of your body.
- Acknowledge the emotion. Give it a label, "This is anger" or "This is fear."
- Continue to focus on your breath as the emotion is present. Be nonreactive, have no judgment of it, just accept that it is there. Be present with it.
- As you continue to focus on your breath, feel the intensity of the emotion reduce as it moves into a state of harmony.
- Move into gratitude now by asking, "Who or what do I appreciate in my life right now?"
- Focus on one aspect in your life that you appreciate most in this moment—a person, a place, a thing—whatever it is. Allow yourself to feel gratitude and appreciation for what they've done for you. You might even choose yourself.

- Continue to breathe in and out as you feel gratitude for the one thing you have identified that you are grateful for right now.

These are just some of the ways you can move emotion through your body to elevate yourself into a better-feeling one.

To live a vibrant life with radical self-love, you must be able to **feel** when you are in or out of alignment with your heart. Radical self-love is the action you take that supports your move to a self-love feeling (an amazing, warm, rich deep, appreciative love). If you are stuck in negative emotion or, even worse, cut off from your emotion like I was, you will never know the feeling of warmth and support that radical self-love brings.

Let yourself feel. Let yourself be guided by those wonderful, nagging, persistent emotions, as they have incredible things to tell you. They tell you:

- how to feel better
- how to empower yourself
- how to be healthier
- how to be loving
- how to move up the scale to joy

Make friends with them. When you lovingly interrupt their pattern and inquire what they want for you, you have a map back to yourself. To empowerment. To radical love for yourself. To vibrant living. And then, with deep appreciation, you can let your new friends go.

Chapter 8

Embrace Your Positive Qualities

"To be beautiful means to be yourself. You don't need to be accepted by others. You need to accept yourself."

– Thich Nhat Hanh

"I just want to stop pressing the "snooze button" on life," said Pam, my new thirty-eight-year-old client who was sad, stuck, and feeling extremely hopeless. "I want to feel like I want to do things, to not have to force myself. I want to stop beating myself up in my mind with negative self-talk and negative behaviors that aren't helping me get into life."

Self-Criticism to Self-Acceptance

Pam was a care home nurse who hadn't been married, had no children of her own, and had experienced only a handful of romantic relationships in her life. "I want to put myself out in the dating world, but I have no confidence and always stop myself before I start."

Pam disclosed she had a mild yet persistent depressive disorder that was affecting everything from getting out of bed in the morning to accomplishing even simple daily tasks. She got herself to work, but that took all the mental and physical energy she had, and there was nothing left for her at the end of the day. She spent most of her evenings watching television or surfing Facebook or Instagram.

She really wanted the energy to just get up and do things where she could feel she was engaging in living.

Her negative self-talk was exhausting. From "Be quiet," "I'm such a burden," "I'll be alone forever," "How stupid am I?" to "Oh my god, I'm worthless," the negative mental chatter was relentless and kept her in a spiral of low-level depression and low-frequency living. For Pam, the inner critic rarely turned off.

First, we worked on her fear. She released a big fear from her childhood related to her parent's disconnected and unhappy union. That fear was lodged in her heart as a big swirling black hole of emptiness where the positive things would be sucked in and never come out. All the anger and sadness connected to this fear that related to wasted time and the message that she would be alone forever was let go of. Pam filled the space with beautiful flowers, each representing a lesson she had learned. She felt lighter.

She cleared two more fear blocks in the throat and solar plexus, moving from "I have to make others happier" to "It's okay to be me."

Pam called me a week later, and she was giddy with excitement. "All week, I felt normal!" she exclaimed. The best was yet to come. "I met a man!" she said, beaming. "I haven't wanted to date in over three years, but something inside me said it was time. I joined a dating app and met Steve." Pam also reported she started putting her clothes away, stopped checking Facebook every ten minutes, and started an exercise routine in the morning. Amazing progress!

Still dating Steve and creating even more positive patterns in her life, Pam came into another session to beliefs. She transformed "I have to be good to be loved," "I have to be perfect," "I have to be quiet" into "It's okay to be me" and "I am perfect as I am." Next, she moved "I can't trust my own mind" and "I can't have my own voice" into "I know what's best for me" and "I deserve love."

Pam identified her positive qualities and all the wonderful things about her from her perspective and the perspective of others. These would move her from **self-criticism to self-acceptance**. Her list went something like this: confident, strong, nurturing, compassionate, fun, caring, and peaceful. Armed with new ways to put her in touch with these wonderful gifts, Pam set off to conquer that mountain and tame the negative self-talk to bolster her self-appreciation and, ultimately, open the door to radical self-love.

The following week, Pam reported that the negative self-talk was so significantly reduced it was almost gone. The more she focused on her positive qualities, the stronger she became, and the stream of negative chatter in her mind got smaller and smaller and then went quiet.

Pam came back to see me a year later. In that year, she continued to keep up the positive patterns (no more Facebook, no more news!), and she grew greater self-acceptance using her positive qualities and feelings. In fact, her list grew and was now huge. It became her default place to live from. She could easily see and experience a positive quality, which brought her joy. It made her stronger. She wasn't with Steve anymore, but as she said, "'I'm not destroyed by it. I chose to leave when I realized it just wasn't working for me. We wanted different things." Pam said, "I feel self-love. I can say with happiness that I love myself. I care about my well-being in a way that I didn't a year ago. I'm motivated and enjoying my life. I know what I want now **and** that I truly deserve it, and I won't settle for less."

Pam worked through and released her blocks, realigned her inner programming, and then shone a light on the positive resources that were always there inside herself, which tamed her inner critic. The space she created by letting go of what she didn't need anymore was filling up with positives: her recognition of her amazing positive qualities. Her positive qualities and positive feelings could now be present, and along with her new beliefs, she was supported in building a rich and empowered life. You can almost feel her vibration rise, can't you? UP she went into a higher vibration of living, and self-love was free to flow in. She could feel it in her heart and was confident in living it.

From Pam's story, you can see how using your positive qualities will build you UP (think higher vibes) and quiet the negative chatter. Negative thoughts are negative energy. And, good news! Low vibration can't live in high vibration. Your positive qualities are your ticket out and up.

Working with the wonderful aspects of you as Pam did will kick open the door to "know thyself." After all, to know me is to love me, right? You can't deeply love someone without first **knowing them well**. My friend, you are not excused from this. Allow yourself to see and work with your positive aspects to get to know yourself well, grow appreciation for all you are, and get your radical self-love flowing.

You don't have to be tortured by self-criticism or berate and belittle yourself into a low self-worth life. Wouldn't you rather feel strong, empowered, and confident and listen to love messages instead of hate bombs? How do you want to feel about yourself? You have choice, awareness, and amazing positive qualities inside of you that will open you up to something better.

Awareness, choice, and positive qualities are a few of the key messages in this fairy tale by the Brothers Grimm. Once upon a time, there lived a beautiful princess. One day, while she was playing with her prized golden ball, she threw it too far, and it landed in the castle pond. The princess was upset and cried as she knew the water was too deep for her, and she thought her prized ball was lost to her.

As she sat by the pond crying, a frog overheard her. "Princess, if I find your ball will you bring me back to the castle, allow me to live with you, love me and allow me to sleep in your bed and eat off your plate?" the frog asked. The princess happily agreed, eager to get her coveted golden ball back.

The frog did as he said and retrieved the golden ball from the depths of the murky pond. The Princess grabbed the golden ball and ran back to the castle, eager to get away from the frog. The frog followed and called out to the princess to remind her of her promise.

The king heard the frog and asked the princess if she had agreed to befriend the frog. She told the king she did, and he told her she must keep her promise.

The frog was happy and accompanied the princess everywhere. He slept in her bed; he ate off her plate. At first, the princess was horrified and disgusted by the frog, but over time she began to grow fond of the little frog and his company.

One day, the princess was overcome with her love for the little frog and lifted him to her lips, kissing him.

At that moment, the frog turned into a beautiful prince. He had been cursed by a wicked witch and needed acceptance and love to return to his human form. The prince and the princess were married and worked together to rule the kingdom for the rest of their lifetime together.

You don't have to kiss any frogs to find your positive qualities. And isn't it nice that we've now moved from swallowing frogs (and burying negativity) to kissing them (and transforming negative into positive)?

In this fairy tale, the princess didn't want to be with the frog, yet when she honored herself and her promise, she found she accepted him and then was able to transform him into her prince.

Okay, no more frogs!

What treasures are hidden in you? Mine these valuable gems inside of you and let yourself sparkle and shine from the inside out. What you shine into your mirror will be reflected back.

Stop for a minute and ask yourself, **"Who am I?"** Now, notice what comes up. Is it that you are a mom, a dad, a lawyer, a doctor, or a caregiver? These are your roles, and while your roles are an important part of who you are and how you interact with life, they are only aspects of you. They are not the *whole* you. Your roles are the parts of you that you show the world—the public or external you.

Who am I? Most of us will answer this with a job title and a list of things we do. Beneath the roles you play, underneath and deeper, you uncover and connect to the true internal you. To move in deeper, look to your **positive qualities** to tell a much richer story of who you are.

Imposter Syndrome, a.k.a. The Imposter Monster

Have you ever felt like a fraud or felt afraid the people around you would find out you really aren't who they think you are? Or felt like your successes were just dumb luck or happened by fluke? If you've felt like this at some time in your life, you have experienced imposter syndrome. Imposter syndrome is a real thing. It's the psychological term that describes when you doubt your abilities and feel an intense internal fear that you will be exposed as a fraud. You will be "found out." Even though there may be a mountain of evidence that shows your capability, competence, and success, still you don't believe in yourself and what you can do. You just can't seem to acknowledge your own accomplishments.

According to *Psychology Today*, over 70 percent of people will experience imposter syndrome at some point in their lives. All you have to do is just google "imposter syndrome," and the sheer volume of articles (6.5 million at the time of writing) shows how pervasive the imposter monster of the mind is.

I think of the imposter monster as the *gap* between how you feel about yourself and how the world sees you. Think about that. If you are not feeling so good about who you are and you can't acknowledge your positive qualities, yet the people around you see you as someone wonderful with a long list of positive attributes, you've got yourself a gap. When the gap is big, the imposter syndrome is big, and you've got some work to move yourself to how the world sees you.

Like a monster inside your head, it feeds on self-doubt and then grows self-criticism and self-judgment. All the negative "selves" are active, and then add in a little fear and anxiety, and you have the perfect environment for feeling like an internal fraud.

The imposter monster plays negative, undermining messages in your mind that create fear. The voice you hear in your mind may sound like you, or it may sound like the voice of someone you know or in some way remind you of them. Through experiences with others, you can easily and unconsciously incorporate their attitudes, values, and qualities, only to hear their voice reflect messages in your mind. Sometimes good, sometimes not so good. Do you ever hear your mother's voice in your head? I carried my mother's voice with me for many years; luckily, it was positive and helped me be safe and grow.

"It's my sisters' voices," Wendy said as she sifted through the negative messages that came at her every day. She was working hard to be a giving, supportive person, a teacher, and a role model to younger women who have been through some of the same terrible traumas and abuses that she had. "When I say hello to a stranger or am kind to someone, I hear their voices say "Look at you sucking up again," or if I am giving or supporting someone who needs it, I hear "You're such a phony," or if I dressed well and am feeling good about how I look, I hear them say "You're ugly." It's definitely my sisters' voices in my head."

Wendy was sixty-five years old and had suffered multiple traumas and violence throughout her childhood and into her early adulthood, the least of which were the abuses and violence inflicted by her three older sisters. Unfortunately for Wendy, her parents were worse. If it weren't for the loving grandmother she could turn to, Wendy would have been completely lost. She went on with life, married three times, each getting progressively better, and had one child. Wendy turned to teaching as a way for her to express care and support for children, a big need in Wendy, and to serve her community.

As she moved through life, Wendy became a competent, intelligent woman who was known in her community as someone you could count on. As a teacher, she was a kind authority figure that would always lend a hand and be there for you. She was well put together and had accomplished many things for herself despite those incredibly difficult early years. With all the odds stacked against her, Wendy had made a success of her life. Yet she didn't feel like a success.

She'd been listening to these voices in her head for decades (her sisters), and each time she heard them, the grip of failure was tightened, and she lived in fear of being a fraud. Wendy was deep into imposter syndrome.

The negative self-talk was holding her in self-criticism and self-doubt, and the only way out was to face them, let them go, and shine a light on her positive qualities to build self-acceptance.

Wendy and I did some work to release the trauma with her sisters (and the others in the family), which brought a great deal of relief. She could relax her body now. She could allow herself to take a full breath. In her mind, Wendy could face her tormentors and express *all* her feelings about the years of negativity and undermining. A tear rolled down her cheek as she said to them, "You never saw the good in me." With all that emptied out of her body, she asked her sisters to leave, "I don't need you in my head," and said, "I deserve peace." And then she watched them go.

Wendy had so many positive qualities to discover. "Kind and compassionate and generous too," she said as she mentally took stock of her positive qualities. She sat up a bit straighter, and a small smile was building. "Strong," she said, "I'm really strong." The words were coming faster now. "Understanding healing because I am healing myself and others." Wendy went quiet and calm, "Lovable," she said. "I'm lovable."

Wendy took those positive qualities and worked with them every day. No longer afraid of being "found out," she became stronger in these positive qualities because she had found herself, and she liked what she found. The occasional habitual negative message popped in, but Wendy quickly interrupted it (with a smile), identified it, and moved to a better thought based on one or more of her positive qualities.

Wendy discovered that the words she used toward herself mattered in her journey to radical self-love. Words, like everything else, have a frequency. The vibration of words and how you choose to string them together will either lift you up or drag you down. You can feel it. Simply put, the words feel good, or the words feel bad. The choice is yours.

Wendy connected with the uplifting vibration of her positive qualities and the words she used toward herself to close the gap and set the imposter monster free. Releasing self-doubt and building self-acceptance through loving words and positive messages that *felt* true and right for her meant that Wendy was aligning herself with her own heart and radical self-love.

Think of the imposter monster as just another way for the body and mind to signal that you are disconnected from your true self and that action is needed to turn yourself around. Your words will make the difference.

Identify Your Positive Qualities

Identifying your positive qualities isn't a terribly difficult thing to do. You don't need to dig deep. Find a quiet few minutes with paper and pen and create a list as you answer these two questions:

1. **Who am I as a person?**

   If you get your roles in life, such as mom, dad, truck driver, etc., go a layer deeper by asking: "**What special or positive qualities do I bring to this role?**"

   Allow your positive qualities to emerge, like Wendy's did: compassion, generosity, understanding, healing, strength, and lovable. As you allow one to come to the surface and show itself, more will pop up, and usually, they will start to show up rapidly.

2. **What is great or unique about me? What makes me special?**

   Each of us is unique in some way, and we all have gifts that make us special. It may be simple, such as being able to easily see the good in people, intuitively knowing when to lend a helping hand, or having a deep connection to nature or animals. It may be more complex, such as being a visionary for future change or being a master of artistry across many areas of your life. Whatever it is, allow them to rise and see your own uniqueness.

If you struggle to answer these questions, you can get your positive qualities from a different perspective. Choose someone in your life who knows you well and that you know loves you. If you are challenged to think of someone, choose someone you work with, a colleague, and make it someone who appreciates you. Imagine your chosen person is answering the questions for you. **What would they say about your positive qualities?**

You now have a list. It may be long or it may be short. It doesn't really matter. It would be best if you aimed for at least three or more. This list of positive qualities is what contributes to your uniqueness in this world. These positive qualities have supported you to grow and evolve and have brought you to this point in your life.

If you are interested in understanding the gap (where the imposter monster lives), change your perspective and answer the questions **as others would answer about you.** If you feel comfortable, you can ask a few trusted family members or friends to provide you with their list of what they experience your positive qualities to be.

Compare your own internal list with the list made from the others' perspectives of you. How far apart are they? Are there any surprises for you from the others' list?

Positive Qualities Hierarchy

With your internal list of positive qualities, you can now put them into a hierarchy or ordered list. The hierarchy tells you what your *core* or **strongest positive qualities** are. As you look across all your life experiences, you will clearly see those one or two top positives, and from there can acknowledge and understand how these have guided and supported you right up to this moment.

To build your hierarchy, compare each quality and decide which one is more important to you or that you feel is stronger inside you.

As an example, we'll use just four of Wendy's seven positive qualities: kind, compassionate, generous, and strong. If you have more than four, as Wendy did, you can continue to follow the process until all are in order.

1. Make two columns on your page and put your internal positive qualities list on the left side of the page. You will move these around according to importance and end up with an ordered list on the left-hand column of the page.

Using Wendy's example, there are four positive qualities on the page and a blank column.

KIND	
COMPASSION	
GENEROUS	
STRONG	

2. The first one on her list was KIND, and the second was COMPASSION.

   I then asked Wendy:

   "Do you feel *KIND* is more important or stronger in you than *COMPASSION*?"

   Move the weaker one to the right column.

   Wendy answered *YES*. KIND felt stronger in her than COMPASSION (but they were close). We moved COMPASSION over to the right-hand side.

   If Wendy had answered *NO*, she would have switched them, and KIND would have moved over.

KIND	COMPASSION
GENEROUS	
STRONG	

3. Next, compare the top left-hand column quality to the one directly below it. In Wendy's case, it was KIND and GENEROUS.

   "Do you feel *KIND* is more important or stronger in you than *GENEROUS*?"

   The stronger one stays in the left column, and the other is moved to the right.

   Wendy answered *NO*. GENEROUS was stronger than KIND. She moved KIND over to the top of the right column, and GENEROUS became the top of the left-hand list.

   If Wendy had answered *YES*, she would continue to compare to see if there was anything stronger than KIND on the list.

GENEROUS	KIND
STRONG	COMPASSION

4. Again, compare the top left-hand column quality to the one directly below it. In Wendy's case, it was GENEROUS and STRONG.

   Do you feel *GENEROUS* is more important or stronger in you than *STRONG*?

   The stronger one stays in the left column, and the other is moved to the TOP of the right.

If Wendy had answered *YES*, she would have moved STRONG to the right, and GENEROUS would have become her top quality in the left-hand column.

Wendy responded *NO*. STRONG was stronger in her than GENEROUS. She moved GENEROUS over to the right column, and STRONG became the top of the left-hand list.

#1 STRONG	GENEROUS
	KIND
	COMPASSION

STRONG was Wendy's #1 positive quality.

5. Now, move the second column over in order underneath your top positive quality.

#1 STRONG	
#2 GENEROUS	
#3 KIND	
#4 COMPASSION	

In Wendy's case, the top positive quality, STRONG, would be her superpower. Her inner strength was the part of her that is her strongest identified inner resource, the supportive force that brought her to this moment. Wendy could now use the tool farther down in this chapter to strengthen the positive qualities lower in the list.

Now that you know yourself on a deeper, more positive level, think back to my earlier question, **Who am I?** How would you respond from this deeper place of your positive qualities? Wendy's response might be, "I am a strong woman whose joy is generosity and kindness, who interacts from a place of deep compassion for all people."

It paints a better picture, doesn't it? It may not roll off the tongue as easily at a social gathering, but this is the essence of who you are. Embrace it.

Now that you know some of your positive qualities, you can notice them in your daily experience. Look back over the last few days and see when these qualities were active and how they were moving you forward.

When you can start to see and then experience those positive qualities that make you uniquely you, this is self-love in *action.*

Affirmations

Words have frequency, and they have power. You know this from the negative words that you've been listening to. Just as negative words have the power to destroy, positive words have the power to heal and transform.

To affirm is to state as a fact, to assert strongly and publicly. Louise Hay, metaphysical lecturer, bestselling author, and creator of Hay House Publishing, points out that "An affirmation is really anything you say or think."

If it's *anything* you say or think, it means you may be affirming positive *or* negative statements, and as you've learned through these past chapters, much of the internal dialogue and beliefs running unchecked are negative. Louise Hay also goes on to say that you must retrain your thinking and speaking into positive patterns with positive words to support positive change, and affirmations open that door.

With affirmations, you consciously choose words that will help create something or eliminate something in your life that will move you to a better state.

Affirmations must be positive, in present tense (in the ***now*** where the unconscious mind lives) and personal, reflecting the change that YOU want. You can't change anyone but yourself, and that means creating an affirmation to change someone else's actions or behaviors won't help you. Another important point is to keep your affirmations attainable. Don't undersell yourself but don't overreach too far, either. An example of this would be to set an affirmation that you are a multi-millionaire when you are currently out of a job and in a lot of debt. Your unconscious mind will reject it as your beliefs around money don't align with being a multi-millionaire at this moment. Do this in stages to move along in attainable ways.

In Louise Hay's book, *You Can Heal Your Life*, she lists hundreds of beautiful and effective affirmations designed to move you from a state of illness in the mind and body into healing.

Examples of positive affirmations are:

> "I am alive to the joys of living."
>
> "I am worthy of all the health, wealth, and love that I desire."
>
> "I deeply love and approve of myself."
>
> "It is safe to shine and be myself in this world."

Affirmations are your positive self-talk; through daily repetition, they become anchored in the unconscious mind and help you alter your thought patterns. Repetition gives it power. The more you hear it, the more you come to believe it and will then act on it.

Remember the reticular activating system in Chapter 4? Affirmations are the targets for your programmable filter and give your unconscious mind a positive target to move toward. And the more you show the unconscious mind what you want (through a positive affirmation), the faster the unconscious mind brings this into your reality.

When you use positive, loving words to build yourself up, you stop the negative chatter and lift your vibration. Another door is opened to radical self-love.

I've created **free bonus resources** for you at www.radicalselflovebook.com, which includes a PDF of fifty self-love affirmations available for download.

How to Embrace Your Positive Qualities

You have your list of positive qualities, and there are several ways to work with them to anchor them and close the gap between how you feel inside and how you are seen by the world (or how you want to be seen).

Eliminating negative self-talk and closing the gap on the imposter monster begins with awareness of the negative message and then the interruption of it so that you can move into a positive message that builds self-acceptance.

When you notice a negative message, take a breath and say STOP in your mind to cut it off. After you have stopped the stream of negativity, there are a few techniques you can use to move beyond it.

1. **Bridge with a Positive Quality or Two**

Look at the message coming at you, and ask yourself, **"What would I rather tell myself?"** Use one or two positive qualities to affirm what is good about you to bridge yourself to a better and more supportive place. You are building a bridge of better-feeling thoughts and messages based on your positive qualities. In the example of Wendy, she heard, "You're such a phony," and from there, after the pattern interrupt to stop the flow, she would say to herself, "I am strong, I am generous, I am kind. Look at how I help others. Look at how I give with an open heart. I can get through anything." She would continue to build this positive story with her positive qualities to turn off the negative message.

2. **Thank You for Sharing**

I was coming through a complete life implosion where everything in my life was upended. In six months, I was separated and heading to divorce after a twenty-three-year marriage. I bought and moved into a new house on my own, my mom died, and my daughter was in and out of the hospital with a life-threatening illness. To top that off, I was given a new work assignment that meant longer hours and a much higher degree of responsibility doing work I hadn't done before. I had limited confidence in what I was doing at work, and it was one of those projects that was a "make or break" your career. Now living on my own and paying for my daughter's care, my job and financial security were at the top of the needs list. Both the stress and stakes were high in my personal and work life.

The mental chatter in my head was on full blast. Some of it was just a stream of things to do: "Remember this, remember that." Yet a lot of it was negative messages based on fear. I just wanted some peace.

I meditated a lot during this time to bring myself into balance and stay connected to my body. I watched webinars and took online courses to expand me spiritually (which I needed amongst the stress). I found a tool that was instrumental in turning off the nonstop stream of negative chatter.

When you have a "run-on" mind, you are not in charge. Your mind is. It's true **you are not your mind**. Think of yourself as the ship's captain and your mind as the first mate. With all that chatter going on, your first mate is running the ship. Somehow you, the captain, have stepped away or are perhaps asleep in your cabin. It's time to get your captain back in charge.

You do this with the simple phrase, **"Thank you for sharing."** When you notice your mind is running rampant or the negative messages are in play, *notice* that it's happening and respond with **"Thank you for sharing."** This little phrase puts you back in the captain's chair (where you should be) and has your mind simply "report to you for duty." It's up to you, the captain, what you do with the information being presented to you. The first mate has been running your ship with no direction, input, or decision-making, just your stunned silence. In the absence of authority and direction, your first mate took over.

"Thank you for sharing."

You, the captain, show respect for the job the first mate has done and for the information being presented. And you signal to your first mate that you take in what's being shared and will decide what to do or not do about it. You take the wheel and begin to steer your ship again.

You may say this fifty times in a day, then it goes down to twenty, and then to ten, and before you know it, the first mate is back under your loving authority and trusts you have it all handled. The chatter stops.

I remember I began this practice sitting on my sofa, wanting to meditate and yet spending my allotted thirty minutes just repeating, "Thank you for sharing." It became a bit of a humorous mantra! As a meditation and mindfulness teacher, I teach this technique to my students because it is so effective. It took a few weeks and some consistency, and then one day, I noticed my first mate was working alongside me in silence.

3. **Daily Affirmations**

Use your positive qualities to build a set of affirmations that expands self-acceptance. In Wendy's example, her top two qualities were **strong** and **generous**. You can also create affirmations for the positive qualities lower in your list to strengthen them.

Create a simple mantra, "I am strong, I am generous," or you can make it a little more complex, "I center myself in my strength and generosity and live my goodness in every moment. All is well."

Follow your breath as you say your affirmations. On the in-breath, you might say, "I am strong," and on the out-breath, "I am generous." Exhale longer on the out-breath to activate the parasympathetic nervous system and signal "relax." This in-mantra, following your breath, also has you focus internally on your body and your breath to calm the nervous system.

Use your affirmations regularly throughout the day. I suggest to my clients that to get into the habit of using affirmations, attach these to something they are already doing, like using the bathroom. Take an extra fifteen seconds in your bathroom visit to run through your positive affirmations.

4. **Use the Reticular Activating System**

The reticular activating system (RAS) brings what you focus on into your awareness. Use the RAS technique to create questions ("what" and "how will I" questions) that fine-tune the unconscious mind and provide a target for your awareness. Create these questions to align with the positive qualities you want to experience more of. **"How will I feel my strength and generosity today?' "How will I experience my kindness and compassion in all I do today?"** You get it.

Use the RAS questions to target any positive qualities you want to strengthen. For example, if you had seven positive qualities like Wendy, you might want to strengthen the bottom three. Design RAS questions to reinforce these specific qualities, **"How will I feel lovable and experience a deeper understanding of myself today?"**

Get curious, get playful, and allow your awareness to show you all of the positive pieces of you that you've been missing.

Feeling good about who you are at a deep level and coming to appreciate your positive qualities moves you deeper into self-love. When you build and strengthen the positive aspects of who you are **to yourself,** your life takes on more positivity and a vibrant richness. You become unshakeable; your resilience strengthens. You get to know yourself, and you love what you see. Your vibration lifts, and you feel expanded in your heart. Your mirror reflects a higher, more vibrant level of living. You experience self-appreciation and even deeper, radical self-love.

Taking steps to get in front of the negative chatter and negative messaging being thrown at you and first turning it down and then turning it off creates a wonderfully peaceful space to build *up* your positive aspects. Let go of self-criticism, self-judgment, and lack of belief in yourself and say *au revoir* to the imposter monster. Identify and work with your inherent, magical positive qualities to build loving messages for you and about you. You will pivot to a new path, an upward path that leads you deeper into radical self-love.

Chapter 9

Be Radical, Put Yourself First

"When we feed and support our own happiness, we are nourishing our ability to love."
– Thich Nhat Hanh

Once upon a time, long ago in the animal kingdom, there was a very beautiful crab. The Creator made Crab very special; he was tall with a big head and beautiful hair, blessed, kind, and rich. Crab was very charitable and giving, making him many friends in the Kingdom.

Crab didn't think about himself; he was happy to give and give. He never said no; Crab felt good and purposeful helping others.

The more Crab gave, the more his friends asked of him.

One day, Scorpion said to Crab, "I would like to move my house to a new place. Crab, can you carry it for me?" Crab was happy to help and moved Scorpion's house.

Snail came to Crab and said, "I must cross the river to get to my home, and the river is full of water, and I can't get across. Can you drink up the water for me?" Crab was happy to help and drank up all the water so Snail could pass easily to his home.

Snake came to Crab and said, "I need a nice place to lay my eggs and raise my children. Can you help me Crab?" Crab left his comfortable home, so Snake could lay her eggs and raise her children.

Next, Lobster came and, knowing how kind Crab was, asked, "I'm getting married, Crab, and I need something nice to wear. Can you help me, Crab?" Crab gave Lobster his best clothes and his gold so that he could go and marry.

Crab had given away a lot, even the clothes on his back, and was sitting on the riverbank deep in thought. Spider approached.

"Crab, I'm in trouble," said Spider. "I must go and see the king, and I must impress the king by thinking clearly and speaking well. Can you help me, Crab?"

Crab replied, "My head is all I have left. I will give it to you so that you can think clearly and speak well to the king." Spider put Crab's head on his own and promised to return Crab's beautiful head later that day.

Spider left wearing Crab's head and went to see the king. The king was very angry with Spider and said, "Spider, you stole my gold, and for that, I will cut off your head." The king ordered his soldiers to cut off Spider's head.

It was Crab's head that was cut off. Spider left the kingdom and wasn't seen again.

Crab waited and waited, but Spider didn't return.

Without his head, Crab couldn't see, he couldn't eat, and he couldn't go out. The Creator saw Crab's dilemma and told Crab, "I will help you with your plight."

The Creator gave Crab a shell to cover his body. He put two short sticks in the shell to be his eyes. He gave Crab a mouth and ears. He gave Crab legs, with two big ones to be his claws. He told Crab to use the claws to nip at anyone who troubled him. The Creator told Crab to use the other legs as his hands and feet.

Crab's friends were afraid of him now and didn't come back to ask him for anything. Crab was now alone.

This African folktale illustrates the dangers and downward spiral of lack of personal boundaries and people pleasing. Without considering self-interests and needs, Crab lost everything. He wound up living in a hard shell with massive claws that nipped at everything that came too close. He swung from one extreme of giving it all away to another, becoming armored and closed off in self-protection.

What would have happened if Crab had learned to put himself first, to say no? What if he had learned to understand his own needs and importance and practiced self-care? Here's what would have happened. Crab would have considered and respected his needs and created boundaries. From there, he would have learned who his true friends were, and ultimately, he would have kept his possessions and his head. He then wouldn't have needed the armor and claws, and he wouldn't have ended up alone in fear and self-protection.

Putting yourself first is self-care and the **foundation of radical self-love**. It means that you consider your own needs and put yourself at the top of the list. You treat yourself with importance and respect and do what's best for you. As a reformed people pleaser, I can tell you I put others ahead of me for many years at my own expense, and was I at the top of the list? Most times, I wasn't even on the list at all.

Putting yourself first is your superpower and puts the "radical" into radical self-love.

Do you always come last? Are you the first to change your priorities to meet the expectations of others?

Check out your Life List. Where do you see yourself on it? Are you first, last, somewhere in between, or not on it at all? Now, look at all the things you put ahead of you. It may be family, friends, work, school, or some other thing you feel is more important than you are.

As Gandhi said, "You can't hurt me without my permission."

You, my friend, are in charge of the list and where you place yourself on it. No one else gets to prioritize that list but you. Acknowledge your needs, wants, and desires and **take action** to protect, nurture and send a love letter to yourself that says, "I know I'm important." It must come from you.

"I have rheumatoid arthritis," Robert said. He had just arrived in my office for his first session. "I'm in constant pain, and it's becoming difficult to walk. I will be faced with hip surgery soon, and I want to see how I can take the inflammation down." Rheumatoid arthritis, a chronic inflammatory autoimmune disease, was slowly spreading through Robert's body, causing him to stiffen up and limit his ability to move. "My life is filled with stress," he said. "I run a busy plumbing business that requires a daily commute. I have two nearly grown children that I support, and I have no help at home. I'm divorced, and the kids live with me."

Robert was sixty years old and facing a difficult decline in his physical health. The stress of his life and the disease were taking a heavy toll.

Throughout his life, Robert had done it all. Literally. He learned at an early age that *giving* kept the peace. He was raised in a trauma-filled alcoholic household, and for him, people-pleasing kept him safe. He took care of the household chores, cooked and cleaned, and helped keep his four younger brothers in line. He found his way out at eighteen when he left home and went up north to apprentice as a plumber.

Once he had his trade, Robert moved across the country, as far away as he could from his family. He was friendly and made friends easily, and he gave much of himself to his friends. He did a lot of free plumbing work too. He started his own plumbing business and eventually met Carol, whom he later married. At thirty-six, Robert was newly married and worked seven days a week as he built his business. He took calls just about any time of day and did paperwork until the wee hours of the morning. When his kids came along, he trimmed his work back to six days a week, but he still worked long hours. He did most of the cooking and spent a great deal of time caring for his kids.

It turned out that Robert married an alcoholic, and his wife Carol went into a spiral of decline. He had to do more at home yet continued in his business with the same workload. Even though he hired additional plumbers, he worked long hours to keep the business strong for his employees.

When Robert and Carol's marriage ended, he found himself at fifty, raising a nine-year-old and an eleven-year-old on his own. Carol was just unable to do it. He moved to a suburb about forty-five minutes away, meaning he had to commute to work and back each day. The stress in his life was really rising now.

Robert continued to "do it all." Cooking, cleaning, working, and caretaking, and by the end of each day, he fell into bed mentally and physically exhausted. He had no time for things that made him happy and spent no time even thinking about what he might want or need. It didn't occur to him to ask others for help or to find ways to increase support for himself. He just kept plugging away. Robert said that just getting through his day was his biggest priority.

He got sick when he was fifty-seven, and even then, it wasn't enough to make him stop and consider what *he* needed. He continued in his pattern of give, give, give, and go, go, go. His decline was rapid, and when he came to see me at sixty, he needed to sell his business and find ways to create space for him to focus on getting well. This meant creating some strong boundaries with his (almost) grown children, to have them participate and help out more, and with himself to make himself a priority. It was now critical.

Robert released fear and trauma, and his programmed limitations. While he was focused on his health, he had a trusted employee run the business and then put it up for sale. Robert did the internal work and, through that, learned to put himself first. He developed new self-care skills and routines, including creating healthy boundaries for himself and his family.

Self-love comprises many things—none more important than acknowledging your inner needs, wants, and desires and putting them first. If the thought of that brings up discomfort in you, there is something in there that needs some tending to.

Putting yourself first does not mean you are selfish. This is an important point, so I will say it again, it is *not* selfish to put yourself on the list or at the head of the line. On the contrary, it is empowering and liberating, and you are meant to experience this.

Consider putting yourself first to be **self-focused,** which we are all meant to be.

You are here to learn, grow, and expand through experiences and relationships. You do that through self-focus. No one else is going to live your life for you (they might try, and you might let them for a time), and the reverse is also true, you can't live anyone else's life for them, no matter how hard you try. As individuals here to experience all there is to experience, it's a self-focused game.

Self-Compassion

Compassion for yourself is about showing yourself kindness and care when there is suffering or misfortune. People who are high in self-compassion treat themselves with kindness and concern when they experience negative events.

The central aspect of self-compassion involves treating yourself kindly when things go wrong. If you were to fail or make an error, as we all do, showing compassion for yourself would mean you treat yourself with extra kindness, care, and reassurance and with less self-criticism, self-judgment, and anger. You would be patient with yourself, show warmth and tolerance, and treat yourself the way you might treat your best friend. This might mean taking time off to give yourself a break emotionally or engaging in positive, encouraging, and forgiving self-talk.

Self-compassionate people are less judgmental and more likely to forgive their faults and inadequacies, and they have less of a need to deny their failures and shortcomings. In fact, people high in self-compassion take greater responsibility for their failures and make needed changes while maintaining a loving, caring, and patient approach toward themselves.

Being compassionate toward yourself creates a protective environment where it is safe to acknowledge any inadequacies and to find ways to improve. You may not have been raised in compassionate environments or circumstances. However, you always have the choice now as to how you want to treat yourself.

Being self-compassionate implies that you want the best for yourself, and it is self-compassion that reinforces and builds self-love.

Increase Your Self-Compassion

Moving into self-compassion requires awareness of those moments you are critical or hard on yourself. In those moments:

1. Treat yourself as you would treat your best friend in this situation. What would you say to them? How would you support them? Offer those positive words and support to yourself.

2. Use mindfulness to allow the emotion to move through you without becoming entangled and stuck in it. See Chapter 7 for a mindfulness exercise on moving emotion.

3. Affirmations (Chapter 8). Create and use positive affirmations that generate kindness, acceptance, and forgiveness:

   "I forgive myself."

   "I deeply love and accept myself."

"I'm going to be okay, and I allow myself to learn and grow from this."

4. Take ten minutes for a self-compassion meditation. Use mindfulness meditation to grow your self-compassion and gratitude.

   I've created **free bonus resources** for you at www.radicalselflovebook.com, which includes three meditation recordings available for download.

5. Recognize you are human and that your experiences, no matter how painful, are part of the common human experience. If you fail, experience loss or rejection, are humiliated, or are in other negative events, even though it feels intensely personal, in reality, everyone experiences problems and suffering. Recognize you are not alone.

Self-Care

Self-care is not a luxury. It's a necessity. To practice self-care means you take care of all aspects of yourself: your physical health, your nutrition, your mental well-being, your relationships, your wants, desires, needs, and connections to the world around you. When cared for and nurtured, all of these things create a vibrant, purposeful life.

When you are out of self-care, your life suffers. And if you aren't going to care for yourself, it's unlikely anyone else will. That job is yours. Letting go of self-care may mean you make others in your life happy (by doing what *they* want) or having more time to juggle a million things, but you are cutting yourself off from YOU, and it puts you out of love and disconnection with yourself.

About twenty years ago, I was at a time in my life when I was doing way too much. I was managing all the aspects of parenting and the kids, working full time, and I was the "business support" for my (then) husband as he started up a new business. I was cleaning my own house, cooking all the meals, making lunches, and restoring a large overgrown garden. When my mom became ill, I took care of her and looked after everything in her life too. A very dear friend took me aside one day and said, "You are responsible for everyone else's lives here. Look at what you're doing. You can't maintain this." She had to say it a few times (and I'm glad she did) because she was right. I was heading for collapse. I was unhappy (and yet totally validated by "accomplishments"), largely unsupported in day-to-day living, and completely exhausted. I developed adrenal fatigue. Something had to change, and it had to come from me. No one else was going to swoop in and save me from me. I needed a crash course in boundaries, and I needed some immediate self-care.

I created a strong boundary for myself around self-care by walking every single day, sometimes two or three times a day. Granted, I got up at the crack of dawn (or even earlier) and walked in the dark with my beloved dog Murphy, and I did it religiously, rain, snow, wind, bears, cougars. It didn't matter. Those walks kept me sane. It was *my* time, and I loved the peace, quiet, and stillness of the dark morning and the companionship of my loyal and, thank goodness, protective dog (bears and cougars!). I worked on my body, taking high-quality vitamins, and I did my best to eat nutritiously. I started reading novels again, which I found to be a wonderful way to set aside the large list of things on the to-do list. I could turn off my mind. I learned to meditate. Most importantly, I learned to say "No," and let me tell you, for me, the people pleaser, that was the hardest self-care practice I had to learn. But I did.

It wasn't always easy for me because the demands in my life were high, and I am a high-energy person. It was a slow adjustment for my family and the folks at work as they were used to my 24/7 availability. I had a really hard time putting down the devices and not answering emails and texts at all hours. Yes, there was pushback. At times lots of it. Saying no felt terrible (at first), and I had to bite my tongue not to undo it. I had to learn to navigate guilt and the "shoulds" I was putting on myself.

Self-care is radical self-love in action. Self-care doesn't mean you are being selfish or don't care about the people in your life who are making demands of you. I think Dr. Phil said, "We teach people how to treat us," which is so true. They will only keep at you as long as you allow them to.

I'm not saying that it's all or nothing or that my self-care was at the exclusion of everything and everyone in my life. It's about balance. Remember, I was a born people pleaser, and that required a conscious shift into **balance** between ME and OTHERS. This is often a tricky start. Like anything you practice, the more I put myself first and saw that the world didn't come to an end, and nobody died because I said no or not now, the easier it got. And then it just became normal.

What areas of your life need a little self-care or a lot of self-care? Maybe it's a daily walk or better nutrition. Maybe it's showing yourself more compassion. Or a spiritual practice like meditation. Self-care could be a day trip to a spa with a friend or just time to have a cup of tea at the end of a busy or difficult day.

Look at your last few days or week even and note how much self-care was present. Was it balanced? Did you stop yourself from doing what you wanted to put someone else first, and if you did, did it feel appropriate? We all have responsibilities and obligations, and there will be times when those things trump you. Emergencies and crisis situations will come up, just as long as your life isn't *always* an emergency or crisis.

When you practice self-care, you build resilience and are better equipped to handle stress. Some research studies show that those who practice self-care (self-love in action) live longer.

10 Tips for Building Self-Care

1. **Put Yourself First**. Set boundaries that allow you to be at the top of the list.

2. **Practice Self-Compassion**. Show yourself the kindness and compassion you would show a good friend in their time of need.

3. **Do Something You Enjoy—Every Day.** Allow yourself some pleasure every single day and do it just for the enjoyment of it. It may be a walk out in nature, enjoying a cup of your favorite tea, reading a chapter of a novel, or a phone chat with a friend.

4. **Take Time for Relaxation.** Allow yourself to detach from stress by taking time to relax. Examples would be daily meditation, a hot bath, reading for pleasure, or getting a massage.

5. **Exercise.** Move your physical body with a walk, a workout, or a yoga routine. Emotion follows motion, so you will be clearing and changing your emotional state too.

6. **Celebrate your Successes.** Notice your successes every day and celebrate them on your own or with others. Celebrate the small and the big successes.

7. **Eat well.** Focus on feeding your body well and with good nutrition.

8. **Increase Social Connection.** Connect with friends and increase your social circles. Spend quality time with the people you love.

9. **Go on a Date (with Yourself).** Take yourself out on a regular date night (or day). Explore new places and interests.

10. **Practice Gratitude.** Make time to focus on the things you are grateful for, no matter how small. When you practice gratitude, you shift your mindset and move into a higher frequency of life. Gratitude is appreciation, which is the number one emotion on the emotional frequency scale (along with joy, love, knowledge, empowerment, and freedom).

I've created **free bonus resources** for you at www.radicalselflovebook.com, which includes a PDF self-care checklist available for download.

Boundaries

Boundaries **are** a key part of self-care as they send a message to your inner self that "What I need matters. I am important," which is radical self-love at its core.

A personal boundary is an imaginary line separating you from something physical, emotional, or related to time or space. These are the lines you draw that state, "Here's where I end and where you begin."

Imagine for a moment that you have a circle around your body that stretches outward about six feet. Imagine the outer edge of that six-foot circle is strong and defined and has the power to keep things out of your circle. The space within the circle, between you and the outer edge, is your personal space. This is what you are in charge of managing.

Another way to look at this would be to think of yourself as the king or queen of a castle. You stand in your court as the sovereign, and there is a deep moat around you protecting you from anything unwanted and those pesky invaders. The drawbridge goes up when you want to keep things out, and you drop the drawbridge to allow things in. You are sovereign, so you get to decide what gets in the castle and how long it gets to stay.

You are the sovereign of your kingdom or circle of personal space.

When standing in a castle, you can easily see where the protective edges are. There are castle walls and a moat that marks where the inner kingdom begins and ends. In your own personal circle, those lines can become blurred. If you don't have a good sense of where your boundaries are (your outer edge), others can come in and just take. And they will.

Boundaries keep you safe, allow you to understand what's important to you and others, and create clear expectations and responsibilities.

They can be physical (*your space and your body*), mental and emotional (*how, when, and who to share your thoughts, ideas, and emotions with*), time (*how you spend your time*), sexual (*consent and safety*), financial and material (*financial resources and how you share material possessions*), spiritual (*your right to believe in and practice what you want*). The final boundary type is called a "nonnegotiable" or "bottom-line" boundary. These are reserved for the things that are complete deal breakers for you, like physical violence or drugs, as examples.

If you don't have clear boundaries in place, chaos can reign, and you may feel stepped on and taken advantage of by others. Anger is often a signal that a boundary (stated or unstated) has been violated and a boundary is needed. Back to my favorite expression, "We teach people how to treat us," and by putting a boundary in place, you are teaching the people around you that this is how it must be if they want to engage with you. As uncomfortable as it can be to establish a new boundary in your life, think of it as a teaching experience.

There are hard boundaries that are unmovable. There are soft boundaries, which are easily moved and dissolved, and flexible boundaries that allow for balance. Ultimately you and the others in your life will have a mix of these types, and understanding what these are will help with your communications.

While working on building personal boundary skills, I didn't imagine I was in a castle with a moat and a drawbridge. I went from the extreme of no or soft boundaries (no protection in place) to the other extreme of super rigid boundaries, where I imagined myself in a bank vault where no one could access me. Oh, it felt good to be in there; it was a mentally peaceful place. But only for a short time. While I felt protected and empowered, I was also closed off, which stopped a lot from flowing in and out. Boundaries are a practice, and eventually, I got much better at navigating what I needed and didn't need and didn't have to go the rigid route for everything. I could be flexible and balanced. I loosened myself mentally and just put a fence around myself in a beautiful garden (although it was tall).

"No is a complete sentence." – *Lee Harris*

Saying no to others can be a difficult thing to do when you haven't had practice. Why is one of the smallest words one of the hardest? When I started saying no, it created a physical reaction in my body. The fear and stress reactions were overwhelming, and my nervous system would flood. It was exhausting.

Along with that, I also felt saying no meant I had to justify *why* I was saying no. I had to have a *really* good reason to say "No" when in truth, you don't. No explanation is necessary. In fact, the more reasons I would give would just provide opportunities for others to try to change my mind or poke holes in my reasoning, which wasn't the point. The point was no. My best friend Shelly told me about a phrase she used that worked like a charm. The phrase was, "That doesn't work for me." She learned it from Wendy, so I give Wendy full credit and my gratitude. It's polite, requires no explanations, and is softer and less charged than a full-out "No." It worked wonders for me as I normalized my internal reaction to the word "No."

What areas of your life could use some new boundaries or strengthening? How would boundaries help with your self-care and support your self-love?

Establishing new boundaries requires a great deal of self-compassion. You won't always get it right, and it won't be perfect. Be kind to yourself as you learn to navigate and communicate your lines. Be patient with yourself, and don't push yourself to go too fast or enter into situations that feel unsafe. Take it slow and recognize this is a new skill you are learning, which takes time and sometimes baby steps.

If your discomfort at working on boundaries is extreme, find yourself a professional to work with who can assist you. A trusted friend, a counselor, a good hypnotherapist, or a healer. You don't have to go it alone.

Boundaries that support self-care are at the heart of expanding the **radical** of radical self-love.

How to Build Boundaries

1. **Do Your Prep Work First.**
   a. Identify the area that needs a boundary.
   b. Identify your outcome. What is it that you want? Why is that important to you (what will it give you)?
   c. Is this a hard boundary or a flexible boundary?
   d. Who do you need to set this boundary with?
   e. Are you ready and able to reinforce this boundary?

2. **Deliver the Message** (in person)

    a. Get yourself into a compassionate and kind mindset before you have the conversation.
    b. Put your feet on the floor so you are grounded.
    c. Breathe. Remember to breathe as you speak so you have a clear head and can think.
    d. State your boundary as clearly and concisely as possible. Avoid too much detail and a list of justifications. You don't have to justify your need, and every justification or reason you provide is an opportunity to be diverted from the conversation (I call this being taken down the rabbit hole).
    e. If they try to talk you out of it, restate it. Explain why it's important to you. Repeat if necessary.
    f. If you are continually challenged, or it becomes emotionally difficult, agree to take a break and come back to it a little later (give it at least a thirty-minute break).
    g. Be compassionate and kind to yourself as you work through this process.

3. **Deliver the Message** (electronically)

    a. Get yourself into a compassionate and kind mindset before you write the message.
    b. Put your feet on the floor so you are grounded.
    c. Breathe. Remember to breathe as you write your message, so you have a clear head and can think.

d. State your boundary as clearly and concisely as possible. Avoid too much detail and a list of justifications. You don't have to justify your need, and every justification or reason you provide is an opportunity to be diverted from the conversation (I call this being taken down the rabbit hole).
e. Give yourself overnight before you send the message, or delete it if it's filled with emotion and start again. Review and edit as needed to ensure the message is kind and compassionate yet outlines what you need.
f. You may get a message back that is emotional or upsetting. Be prepared for this.
g. Respond in the same way, keeping the emotion out of it, and restate. Explain why it's important to you.
h. If you are continually challenged, or it becomes emotionally difficult, agree to end the discussion. Consider a conversation if that is comfortable for you.
i. Be compassionate and kind to yourself as you work through this process.

Putting yourself first says to you, the people around you, and the world, **"I matter,"** and isn't that what you want? To be seen for who you truly are? To feel like you matter, that you are valued and cared about as the sovereign of your own castle? Nothing builds your own sense of worth and creates empowerment faster than this. When you matter, life opens up, and you notice more good feelings than bad. You shift. Your frequency naturally lifts, and life takes on a vibrant magical quality that just keeps growing.

Loving self-care, healthy boundaries, and putting yourself first will not only empower you, but it will also show others who you are. You are not a background player. You are not someone who is here just to serve. You are not someone to live a monotonous, boring, unfulfilling life. You are the star of your own play, a magnificent person with hopes, dreams, and desires. And when you consistently and lovingly make time for yourself to explore, care for yourself and do the things that bring pleasure and joy, you deepen your self-love and show the way to others.

Radical self-love requires action, and this is it. This is where you make your self-love extreme.

Chapter 10

Go Beyond, Build a Higher Connection

"There is a voice that doesn't use words. Listen."

– Rumi

The chair was hard and cold, and I could feel the chilled air on my face and my feet. Despite wearing heavy layers, the cold seeped in, and I knew that the old gymnasium wouldn't get any warmer today. I'd been sitting in this chair off and on now for a few hours and with a group of people I didn't even know. I was at a day-long Hawaiian meditation and healing retreat, and I was waiting for my Higher Self to show up.

The leader, our "Huna" for this retreat, said, "When you connect to your Higher Self, and it is present, you will feel warmth flow in. You will feel love and expansiveness."

Oh yes, I was ready for this. We'd been meditating throughout the day for what felt like hours, and although I could focus on each meditation, I hadn't made a connection yet. He continued to guide us in meditation, and just as I was giving up near the end of the practice, she came. And he was right. It was like nothing I had felt before.

I'd been searching for "more" my whole life, for as long as I could remember. It became a conscious and purposeful quest once my life imploded in 2012 with my challenge year, when my marriage ended, illness and death struck two family members, and my career took a turn. These challenging months (or a full year in my case) are designed to force one into transformation, to move a person in a new direction. *To wake you up to yourself.* Well, I was completely picked up and plunked down, facing in a completely different direction. This was an enriched "wake-up" year for me.

This was about connecting to my own true self, my spirit. Now, I'm not talking about religion, and if spirituality is an uncomfortable topic, I invite you to move on to the next chapter. But before you go, I would like to say that spirituality, for me, is a conscious recognition that you are more than just a body. There is more to you than this. And now I ask you, do you feel that too? Do you feel there is a life force inside you that propels you forward and grows and expands with every experience you have? That's what I'm talking about.

This chapter will be about as out there as I get in this book, with the concept that you are more than your body and the other part of you that exists outside of your body, your Higher Self (or soul), is an incredible resource available to you.

William Buhlman, an incredible teacher of the exploration of consciousness that I have had the pleasure of learning from, says in his and his wife Susan Bulhman's book *Higher Self Now!* "It is our essential core, that which has guided us through all of our lives, supporting our present education on Earth, and preparing us for our infinite journeys. It is the very **heart of our being** that knows our strengths, limitations, and aspirations. It is the part of us that recognizes the unseen purpose for all of our experiences."

I'd heard about the Higher Self, and in my quest to know myself better, I wanted to understand and connect to this part of me and get to know it better too. What would it feel like, and how could we work together?

I'd spent a few years searching for that deeper connection, and on that grey and drizzly afternoon, sitting on the hard, cold, uncomfortable chair at the end of the retreat, it happened. After years of trying, in she came (I think of her as she; you can think of your Higher Self in whatever way works for you), and it was true—it was a gentle feeling of warmth flowing into my body from the top of my head down to my heart. I felt expansive in my heart, like I would burst out of my body. This was bliss, and it was completely blissful to be connected to this wonderful larger part of me.

This feeling of ME was like nothing I had ever felt before. My heart felt full and radiant as I sat in that feeling of bliss and deep love. There was no doubt at all: I was loved, accepted, seen, and supported—all in about three minutes. And then BOOM! The meditation was over, and the connection was gone. I definitely wanted more of that, and I knew that three minutes of bliss was worth the cost of the whole retreat.

This is the deep well of love that exists through your Higher Self, your soul energy, your true you. When you take the time to open that connection, this feeling of bliss and completeness is present inside of you. And it never goes away. Well, the bliss part moves up and down, but your sense of wholeness, authenticness, and deep knowing yourself is always with you. Your self-love is radical.

Do you feel complete, or do you feel like you are missing or yearning for something or someone? When you tap into your heart and think about yourself, do you get a warm, expansive feeling?

You don't have to make a connection to your Higher Self and invite it more deeply into your life. This is a personal choice. You can just carry on moving through life as you have been. Even if you follow the steps and ideas as outlined in this book but skip this part and put yourself first, you will build deep appreciation and love for yourself. But I ask you, **Do you have room inside for more? Do you want to go deeper?** Check in with your heart. Does it want more?

What if your Higher Self was your soulmate? Soulmates have been around for a long time and are as old as the ancient Greeks. Way back when, back in the 300s, at Plato's Symposium (a drinking party with speeches), he and a bunch of other philosophical men like Socrates, Pausanias, Aristophanes, and Agathon, got drunk and gave their ideas and opinions on love. In part of the Symposium, Plato orated about soulmates.

One of the speeches by Plato addressed the idea from mythology that two people come from one. The Greek myth goes that Zeus, the almighty God of the Gods, was afraid that the humans who were physically perfect and becoming more powerful would turn against him. He could have struck them all down with thunderbolts, but he was afraid to lose his tributes and wanted to be worshipped. Zeus split humans in two, creating a male and female counterpart. It not only made them weaker but also doubled the population, which meant the offerings and worship of the Gods would double.

The separated humans would now be condemned to spend their entire lives looking for "the one," their other half, the spiritual, physical, mental, and emotional pieces that would make them feel whole again. It would be a burning desire to seek and yearn for that completeness of self.

What if your Higher Self, your soul energy, was your other half? The seeking you do for another human can't fill the void within you that the disconnection from your Higher Self (your true other half) creates. Rather than seeking externally and, as the song goes, looking for love in all the wrong places, what if you looked *inside* yourself and invited the other half of you ***in*** to fill, nourish, and create with you? Then you would not only feel whole, but you would *be* whole. And that is what you would offer of yourself in all your human relationships. You would be offering the whole you rather than a half of you. The real you.

Think about this. You are the only person in your life that will ever really know the authentic you, from the very start of your life right up to this moment as you read these words. No one else knows your full journey but you. Your Higher Self, your other half, knows every second of your journey here and knows you even better than that. It knows your whole existence as a soul, across all of your lives and outside your lifetimes. If it knows you best, why wouldn't you build that partnership and make your life shine?

Hang on now. Here's where we go a little out there. Are you ready?

When you come into a body, you don't bring all your energy with you, it is too much, and your body can't hold it all. You leave a large part of your soul energy out in the higher planes, and that's the part we all know as your Higher Self. It's your soul energy that stays in energy form rather than inhabiting a body, and it loosely oversees your time here on Earth, ensuring you don't veer too off course from the path you set for yourself. Yes, your life has a greater plan. These two parts of you, your Higher Self as the dynamic, growing life force consciousness, exists outside the body, and your everyday "in the body" consciousness is just an *aspect* of your Higher Self. Your Higher Self is a slightly dormant energy, loosely hanging around about three feet above your head, not interfering (except maybe in an emergency). You have to "wake it up" out of its dormancy to get the partnership going.

Your life force, your soul, your Higher Self is LIGHT, beautiful soul love LIGHT that shines through you. Have you met someone whose eyes sparkle and shine? What you are seeing is their life force shining through. The expression is true, "Your eyes are the windows to the soul." You can see a lot if you stare deeply into your own or someone else's eyes.

When you let go of the dense, heavy energies created here in emotional situations (the fears, the blocks, the traumas, the limitations, and wounds), you can hold **more LIGHT**. More of your own LIGHT shines through. Have you noticed that when you release something heavy in you, you feel physically lighter? You shine more. The process of releasing the dense, heavy energies to bring in more light **is enlightenment**—to carry more light—which is our collective goal.

I have another dear friend (I am very blessed with dear friends) who was doing her yoga teacher training a few years ago. This was an intense, year-long process that required weekly training, multiple yoga sessions each week, and lots of meditation. Plus, homework—more meditation and yoga. She meditated at least twice a day. Although we talked on the phone often, I hadn't physically seen her for a few months. We decided to meet for a well-deserved lunch and catch up. I watched the door for her arrival and who should walk in but this beautiful, radiant, light-filled woman. My friend was stunning, and I could easily see she was carrying much more of her own light. She told me that in her coursework, she was shedding dense energies; the blocks, traumas, wounds, and the meditation multiple times every day had created this incredible warm glow in her. She now craved this connection and spent time sitting in it, feeling it filling her up and carrying her through her day. Strangers stopped her on the street just to say hello, make a kind comment, or even tell her she was beautiful. She was being seen because she carried more light! The connection was made to her Higher Self, and in carrying more light, she shifted into a higher frequency of living where life felt amazing.

The empty "seeking to fill" feeling is only filled with what light you have embodied. More light comes from your Higher Self when you create the room by shedding the dense low-vibration energies. When you connect and nurture your Higher Self relationship, as my friend did through her yoga and meditation practice, your need to seek goes away, and the empty heart fills. You aren't looking for others or for substances or situations to fulfill you because your own light fulfills you. You are in a relationship with your perfect soulmate, and you become a *whole* being. There is no self-love deeper than this. This takes radical to a whole higher level.

Your Higher Self is a part of your life whether you decide to connect and work with its radiant heart-centered and soul-based love and support or not. It's a choice you and you alone make under the laws of free will as you navigate your life in a body. Your Higher Self knows all about the challenges in your life, the learning to be gained, and your general life plan. It is the very essence of who you are and has all the accumulated knowledge across all your existence. Your Higher Self has no limits and is the wise teacher within you. It communicates to you through your heart, higher intuition, and feelings and by sending you odd coincidences and synchronicities. It is an incredible resource of guidance, wisdom, and understanding.

When you return to self-love and then let your Higher Self in, you have access to higher levels of intuition, insights, revelations, and expanded awareness. And why wouldn't you want that?

Work with Your Higher Self

To wake up your Higher Self and get this larger part of you actively working with you, your Higher Self needs an invitation. It will never interfere with your free will and sovereignty as the creator of your life, so you must request its presence and make it known it is welcome.

Every day take five or ten minutes to sit quietly in meditation. Invite your Higher Self, *out loud,* to come around you. "Higher Self, come around me now; help me to feel you with me." Allow yourself to feel the energy in your body and around you. Within a short time, perhaps a few days or weeks, or even immediately, you will feel a shift in your energy field as your Higher Self connects. Focus on your energy field and notice the subtleties of change during this practice.

Your Higher Self as a Creator

Now you can ask your higher self to help you to **create** whatever it is you want to create. This is your true partner in creation, and when you are working together, the creation is rapid and rich! "Higher Self, come around me now; help me to feel you with me. Create with me a day of ease, a day of bliss. Create an uplifting and magnificent day."

Expand Your Heart

Once you are good at feeling the connection, you can then invite your Higher Self (out loud) to come into your heart, into your body. You will begin to *feel* your Higher Self inside and the warmth and expansion in your heart. Your heart is the seat of your soul, and it will feel *full.* This is where your expansiveness is and where your light radiates. "Higher Self, come around me now, and come into my body, into my heart. Help me to feel you with me. Create with me a glorious day, a day of love, a day of healing, a day of ease and flow."

Ask for Guidance

Now that the relationship has been established and you can feel the depth of your soul's energy and expanded heart, you can ask your Higher Self for guidance. "Higher Self, come around me now, and come into my body, into my heart. Help me to feel you with me. What do you, my Higher Self (or soul), want me to know today?" Wait for the answer to pop into your mind. If you have a specific question, you can ask, "What does my Higher Self want me to know about [insert your concern]?" (i.e., health, love, situation, etc.).

The answer will be **loving and supportive**, <u>never negative</u>. If you get something that feels negative or not loving, then it's not a Higher Self answer. Ask again and let that message pop in. You will quickly learn to discern what's coming from your Higher Self and what's coming from the conscious mind or fear.

Another way to do this is through automatic writing. This is where you have a piece of paper and something to write with. Ask your question and allow the words to flow through you onto the paper without consciously creating them.

Bring Power and Light into Your Body

Your Higher Self can bring more light and power into your body just by asking. "Higher Self, come around me now, and come into my body, into my heart. Please bring as much light and power as I can hold in my body today." As you clear away the denser energies, you will be able to hold more of your power and light, and in the process, you will raise your frequency to a higher level of living.

A daily connection and invitation to your Higher Self to create and communicate with you wakes it up and wakes YOU up to your whole and true self. You have a deeper, solid, stable love for yourself in your heart that you can count on. You expand and radiate your inner light from your heart into the world. You know yourself better, and you feel strong about who you are. You live from a higher vibration and create on a grander scale. You grow through positive and consciously self-directed experiences. You live a vibrant life.

When you work with your Higher Self to make your self-love radical, there is no more clinging pains, emptiness, and seeking. Just a beautiful deep sense of self and self-acceptance remains, an expanded love and appreciation for the whole of you, which makes YOU vibrant and unshakeable.

Chapter 11

Radical Self-Love Blooms

"Knowing yourself is the beginning of all wisdom."
– Aristotle

Know thyself. This is the underlying theme through all the steps in this book that allows your radical self-love to come out of hiding and elevate you.

You've covered a lot of ground across your greatest geography, the map of YOU. Through your compassionate exploration of that territory and leaving no stone unturned, you now know yourself better, deeper, and understand your true self. **Radical self-love blooms**.

You can follow one or two of the steps and create a better feeling experience, but when you take *all* the steps, something magical happens. Your awareness opens. You know what you want, and you're confident and excited to go out and get it. You put yourself first, and it's empowering! You feel positive about life. You live in a greater state of harmony and flow and live life from a higher vibration. You step into your penthouse!

When that magic happens and radical self-love blooms, you are assertive about who you are, and you know you can accomplish anything! When bad things happen (and they will), you can handle them. You know your strength, and you feel it. You are unshakeable, and your resilience grows. The stresses of life become smaller. Your deep appreciation for yourself and the connection to the whole and true you now radiates from your heart and affects everything in your life. Your relationships improve, and yes, you feel lighter and you smile more.

Life unfolds in beautiful and vibrant ways.

"I am doing so well!" Rachel exclaimed. Her eyes sparkled as she stepped into my office. "It finally feels like I'm the one driving my life, and I'm on this amazing journey. I started a school program that I know is the right path for me, and I can feel it. I left my boyfriend, who I discovered wasn't good for me, and you know me, in the past, I would have stayed *way* too long and brought myself down. And the big news is that I let go of my dad. I realized I just couldn't have a relationship with him, and I am so happy to stop trying. I *finally* understand the importance of *me*, and now I put myself first and feel love for myself. I know I deserve a better life." Rachel was back for some energy work to balance her body with all the changes she'd recently made. She was animated and beaming as she took me through her life changes in the past few months. "I can't thank you enough for the work we did and your help in getting me here."

When I met Rachel a few months earlier, she really wanted her life to unfold in beautiful and vibrant ways, but unfortunately, it was not. She was thirty-eight, working in a job she hated with toxic people. She had recently relocated to my city to escape the bad romantic relationship experiences she'd had. She suffered from anxiety, which went extreme through her experience with COVID-19 and isolation. She drank too much and told me she had PTSD from her childhood. As a self-proclaimed derailer, Rachel had become aware of her pattern of sabotaging the good things in her life, and now she was having some physical issues. Rachel was on a downward spiral, being pulled farther and farther away from her own self-love.

"I want to stop attracting negative people into my life, and I want to stop worrying. I want to accept myself, love myself, and feel kindness toward myself," she said. "If I love myself, then I know I will feel more grounded, loved, and respected by the people around me. That's important to me."

She started with the unresolved trauma and fear. The trauma held her tight and was so good at protecting her that it blocked her from receiving and allowing good things in. She released the traumas and fears and cleared a lifelong issue with her throat related to fear about feeling her own value. It prevented her from speaking out and having a voice because the fear was, "No one will believe me." With that gone, a deep fear in her heart surfaced. It was dark and black, and that felt like hate from her dad, who had been telling her since she was a young child that she was difficult and exhausting. She released that with the understanding that it wasn't her fault and she didn't have to believe her dad's negative messages.

After this level of unresolved trauma and fear release, Rachel felt incredible. "The PTSD response is gone," she said at her next session, "and I'm not afraid of COVID-19 anymore. Another thing, I have no desire for alcohol, and I don't feel like my nervous system is wide open all the time. I feel grounded more often." Rachel had made some great strides in letting go of the barriers to her own self-love.

Next up for Rachel was working on the limiting belief systems and negative patterns playing out and holding her hostage. We uncovered her core belief of "I'm not worthy," which had been running in her life since she was a young child. Having been repeatedly shamed and laughed at by her dad and grandma, she took in that "Love isn't safe. Men aren't safe. I don't matter. I'm not lovable." All were attached to the core belief that **"I'm not worthy."** Once that was locked in, life took on some difficult twists and turns for Rachel, and the negative patterns (especially with men) were running. She moved "I'm not worthy" to "I am lovable and perfect as I am" and collapsed the supporting beliefs. The negative pattern with love told her to learn to ***trust herself*** and ***listen.*** Rachel built a solid awareness around her patterns that allowed her to practice self-trust and really listen to herself.

Right after her session, she was able to strike up a conversation with a nice man, as she put it, without panicking inside. She said it felt natural. She had no expectations of this conversation going anywhere (it didn't), but it was incredible to her to have such a pleasant experience and be able to speak with a man without freaking out inside or feeling her nervous system move into high alert.

More was coming up for Rachel. Suppressed emotion, long buried, was making its way to the surface to be looked at, learned from, and discarded. "I haven't thought about my first boyfriend in years," she said, "but there he was. He just popped into my mind when I was out walking. I remembered how bad I felt when he left me. I was completely gutted. I thought he was the love of my life."

The "gutted" feeling was telling her to *trust herself*, *be herself*, and *tap into her intuition*. She could see the red flags in the relationship, but she chose to ignore them and ignore her own needs. With the emotion's learning and gift in place now, she was able to let it go.

What Rachel noticed next was the negative self-talk and how she was catching it as she was saying negative things to herself. Her positive qualities (powerful, free, loving, strong), affirmations (I am strong, I can get through anything, I trust myself), and some tapping shut down the negative self-talk.

Rachel changed jobs twice. She left those toxic people and moved herself into higher financial positions and more responsible positions that allowed her to learn. She was lifting her frequency. She still wasn't crazy about the work, but the situations were working much better for her now, and she was learning. She talked about going back to school.

One of the big things that Rachel could now do for herself was cement her feelings of worthiness and value through firm boundaries. Rachel explained, "For years, I tried to make it work with my dad. I was always bending and twisting myself to fit what worked for him. One day I just decided, 'I can't do this anymore. I'm worth so much more than this,' so I closed the door on having him in my life. In some respects, it is sad for me that he has never really wanted to know me, the real me, but I see clearly now that's *his* limitation, not mine. He's stuck in his own story, and I just can't be a part of it."

She also broke up with a recent boyfriend that just didn't feel good anymore. Rachel had learned to put herself first.

Putting herself first meant she had to know what she wanted. And she knew she definitely didn't want the profession she was in. She quit her job and signed up for school, following her passion into a nature-based meditation and therapy program that filled her with great joy, hope, and excitement for her future.

"I meditate every day and connect with my Higher Self," Rachel said, "and I feel whole. I can feel it in my heart and my whole body. There is an energy running through me that is incredible. I just feel so much gratitude for being here, feeling this good, living my adventure."

Rachel turned her whole life around, shedding the past and creating room for her goodness to shine through. She lifted her vibration to a higher frequency of living. Her heart opened. She knew who she was and where she was headed. She felt full and fulfilled. Was it perfect? Would it ever be perfect? No life story is ever perfect, but she had the radical self-love to move through whatever would be thrown at her. She believed in herself, appreciated herself, and was loving to herself. One thing she really wanted when we met was a solid love relationship. She didn't have that romantic relationship yet, but she did have a solid love relationship with herself now. And that's where a vibrant life begins.

What the stories I've shared with you throughout these chapters have in common is the deep **desire to change** something to feel better about self and live a more heartfelt life. For Rachel, immediate relief meant dealing with the unresolved trauma and PTSD response. I don't know which of the areas I've outlined in this book will bring you immediate relief but trust yourself to know that you know. Look through the chapters and allow yourself to feel which areas of this book are "charged" for you. That's right, use your emotional guidance (Chapter 7). That charge means something underneath needs exploration and change. It's a wound. If you've done the self-inquiry and discovery work through the chapters, have a look again and "check your charge." Go back and revisit whatever might be left.

The easiest place to start on this journey is with your mindset and opening your awareness to **what's really going on** in your world. Awareness is the fuel of change's fire, and you won't move in any direction without it. Your mindset tells the story of how you create in your life and whether you choose to live a high-frequency life (moving up to the penthouse) or a lower-frequency life (down on the fourth floor or even lower). If there is one thing you need to focus on that will pave the way for dramatic change, it's your mindset. Radical self-love can't happen from a negative place.

Personally, I like to see my progress. I find it motivates me. If that's you too, I suggest you explore your positive qualities first before doing anything else. Once you have your list, you can gauge how they are changing, what's being added, and how they grow as you go through the steps in this book. You will notice what you are adding. I think of this one as **eating your dessert first** and getting all the good stuff up front.

If you are a spiritual person, you can do the work on connecting to your Higher Self up front too. This part of you is who knows you best, so why not make the journey together? I think of this one as having your **spiritual support team** with you, which creates the potential for doing work at an even deeper level.

This book is laid out as a series of steps, with each step building on the next. You may or may not need to do all the steps. Perhaps you've already done a lot of personal growth work and just need some tweaks. Maybe you are weak in beliefs but are great in boundaries. Whatever it is you need, set aside some time for yourself each day to focus on YOU and your inner journey. And, of course, this counts as part of your self-care practice (Chapter 9).

Get yourself a journal where you can write down your ideas and map out your thoughts and experiences. You don't have to keep the journal if you don't ever want to revisit your writing. I do a ceremonial burning of my journals as a symbolic (and physical) way of letting it all go, but I do know people who have a huge collection of their journals that go back years, even decades. That's just not my style. When I'm done with it, I let it go. Whatever you choose, the act of writing brings it out from your head and shines a light on it. It creates awareness. And when it's in physical form, written down right in front of you, you have an opportunity for clarity.

Picture this as the journey to radical self-love. Imagine your awareness as a hallway with hundreds of doors to choose from. A positive mindset will get you to the right door. In front of the right door, your trauma and fears pop up and block you. Clear those, and your limiting beliefs stop you from turning the door handle. Change those, and your negative patterns don't allow you to push the door open. Transcend those and watch the door swing open wide. Step through the door and be greeted by a wall of your suppressed emotions. Give them their due and take all the learning they have for you as the wall crumbles. Your heart stirs. Notice your positive qualities growing on either side of the path as you move forward. Pick the ones you want to carry with you. Your heart opens. You may notice others stepping onto your path who try to pull you in a different direction. With your open heart and positive qualities, you stand strong, and you put yourself first. Your heart grows bigger. You move ahead with healthy boundaries in place. As you walk, you care for yourself. You notice how wonderful you are and feel compassion and appreciation for you on this journey. You feel worthy. You deserve to be on this path. On your journey, your Higher Self joins you. You are radiant. You are whole. Your heart is full. You are in radical self-love.

The journey is yours, and as Lao Tzu so aptly put it, "The journey of a thousand miles begins with a single step." Luckily this isn't a thousand-mile journey. You can start your journey at the very beginning, eat your dessert first with your positive qualities, bring in spiritual support, or just start from where you are. The important thing is to start *somewhere.*

Radical self-love is for everyone. You don't have to be "special" to love yourself and live a vibrant life. Everyone is special. Yes, you are too! Marina, Kathy, Robert, Bonnie, Pam, Rachel, and all of the people I've shared stories about (and me!) are just ordinary people, like YOU, who wanted more for themselves and were willing to look inside and do some shifting. You can too.

Everything you need for radical self-love and living vibrantly is inside you.

It took me a lot of years and a lot of experimenting with different ways to achieve radical self-love, and I did it. I live a vibrant life. My vibrant life might not look the same as yours, and that's okay. We all have our needs, wants, and desires based on our individual purposes and paths.

My journey was filled with twists and turns and took many years. I want you to get there *much* faster with the wind in your sails and the sun on your face.

Chapter 12

Your Vibrant Life

"Open your heart, ignite the flame in your being and awaken the natural flow of life energy in your heart. When your heart opens, the world around you changes."

– Mingtong Gu

When you picked up this book, you knew you wanted more for yourself. You wanted to feel better in some way. No, let's correct that. You **needed** to feel better in some way because your status quo was no longer sustainable. Something might very well break, and you realized it could be you. Living disconnected, not tapping into your value, **your own heart,** meant living with lower self-esteem and lower self-worth and the host of difficulties and issues these create across all aspects of your life. Perhaps it was a job that wasn't fulfilling, a string of bad relationships, financial issues, or struggling with your weight or physical health. Whatever those issues were, they were affecting you at your core, leaving you unfulfilled and suffering.

This was your wake-up call.

I asked at the beginning of this book, **How much time do you have?** How much of your life has been lived from this place of disconnection and lack? Life is short; it truly is, and you don't want to waste another minute. There is an urgency for all of us to move inward and get to know and love ourselves so that we can elevate our lives and shine brighter in the world. And the more you allow yourself to shine, you are teaching others how to shine their light too. Every step you take through the chapters of this book will peel off the heavy layers and create space for your light and the goodness of your true self and radical self-love to shine through.

When you let go of the past, the stories, the traumas, the wounds, and the programming, you open the door to the deep well of love and appreciation for yourself. When you make loving yourself your first priority and live from the top of your list, everything around you changes. It's the key to a happier, more fulfilled, and deeply connected life. You love better. You can handle stress and are more resilient to the bumps and bruises of life. When you live from radical self-love, you naturally lift your frequency to a higher playing field, and life unfolds in beautiful ways.

You want to live a life that is positive, empowering, and vibrant, right?

"I am uplifted now. I feel expanded, and my heart feels warm," Bill said in response to our last session together. "I feel like I am loving myself again. I can appreciate me. I can be kind to me. I never knew that life could feel like this. I'm amazed at what's inside me."

Bill was seventy-seven years old and wanted to clear out what had been weighing him down for years. He had metastasized cancer, struggled with negative thinking and anxiety, and wanted to be more accepting of situations. A single man, Bill had never married and retired from a distinguished career in the military.

We followed the process to get to radical self-love.

Bill cleared out trauma and fear that had been present since early childhood, unresolved and creating panic, feelings of being inadequate, and guilt. He had felt alone since the age of sixteen, and that was a root of anger and confusion that held him back and reminded him to be careful, be aware. This hypervigilance had been running for over sixty years. It was exhausting. He changed his programming and removed "I am not worthy of love," "I'm not good enough," and shifted into "I am lovable," "I am accepting," "I am enough," "I am worthy of a good life." He allowed his suppressed emotions to surface, and with mindfulness practice, he gently let them go. He understood their messages.

Bill had some amazing positive qualities—seventy-seven years of them. The challenge was he could see a few but not a long list that would sustain him. He brought up joyfulness, strength, resilience, compassion, confidence, and trust that he could then use as his path to his true self. He used his affirmations ("I am worthy of understanding, I have love in my heart for others and myself, I learn, appreciate, and move on"). And finally, Bill made the connection with his true self, his Higher Self. Bill was a meditator and practiced meditation for years. He was a very spiritual person, and adding the one practice to bring in his Higher Self not only improved his meditation practice but fully opened his heart. He felt uplifted and expanded and could feel the goodness in his heart for himself. At seventy-seven years old, Bill had reached radical self-love.

It's never too late.

Let's look at the big picture. It only takes four steps to move into radical self-love. That's it, just four. Depending on where you stand in your life, some steps might be bigger than others, but nonetheless, it's just four.

The first is to **change what's inside.** Dr. Wayne Dyer, an internationally renowned author and speaker in the field of self-development, tells a wonderful metaphor about an orange that you can find published across the internet and in YouTube videos. I'm going to share this with you because it illustrates how you've been living and how the choice of self-care changes what's inside you. As a motivational speaker, Wayne spoke to large audiences, and often he would bring out an orange to make a point about what's inside of us. As he tossed the orange between his hands, he asked the audience what would happen if he squeezed the orange as hard as he could. What would come out? The audience responded, "orange juice." Wayne then asked them if he could get apple or grapefruit juice from the orange. The audience responded with a quick and loud "NO" amid much laughter. He went on to reference a conversation with a young girl at a previous event, where he asked her why, when he squeezed the orange, could he only get orange juice? He said the girl thought about it for a second and answered, "Because that's what's inside."

Wayne then told the audience to extend the metaphor and think of the orange as YOU. While holding up the orange, he said, "Assume someone squeezes you and says something you don't like. Someone behaves toward you in a way that you find offensive. Someone does something to you or says something to you that you feel hurt by. And out of you comes anger, hatred, bitterness, tension, fear, anxiety, and stress. And immediately, you say, "That comes out of me because of the way he said it," or "the way that she said it," or "the way they did that." The truth and reality is what comes out is what's inside. And if you don't like what's inside, you can change it. It's *up to you.* It's your choice."

This is the first step, deciding and choosing what you want inside you. Will you react with love when you are squeezed or something else? Change what's inside your mindset, let go of fear and limitation, and make friends with your emotions. When you change what's inside, you begin the journey of moving yourself to a higher frequency of living, and you are on your way to the penthouse.

The second is to shine a light on your positive qualities. Even if you have to be on high beam to find them (we can bury them deep), you will bring these to the surface and get reacquainted again. And you will build more. Would you fall in love with someone if you didn't see anything good about them? I hope not. The same holds true for you. How can you feel love for yourself if you can't recognize the positive in yourself? Move yourself from self-criticism to self-acceptance, and as you lift yourself closer to your own heart, you shift yourself again into higher-frequency living.

The third is making yourself the star of your own show by putting yourself first and prioritizing self-care. You become the star by nurturing yourself—the most important person you know—and by setting healthy boundaries with others so that you protect and manage who and what gets into your inner kingdom. That choice is yours. Really!

The fourth is connecting your heart to your true self, your Higher Self, and living every day from a deeper place of trust and love. You are supported by the one who knows you best, your soul, and bring even more compassion and love to your everyday experience when you open up to and work with your Higher Self. You've left the fourth floor and are truly living in the penthouse now. You make your self-love radical by putting yourself first, drawing your love, support, and compassion from you at the soul level.

You may have already been working on changing what's inside you, or you may be starting at the beginning of the road. The key here to all four steps is **awareness.** When you become aware, you have what it takes to move through these steps and become who you were meant to be, not someone else or the world's idea of who you are, but your true lovable self.

There is an Indian fable from the nineteenth-century Hindu guru Ramakrishna called *The Tiger and the Goat* that highlights the importance and power of self-awareness. A tigress was pregnant and starving when she came across a flock of goats. With her last ounce of energy, she pounced but fell short of her goal of killing a goat and collapsed in weakness. She gave birth to her cub and then died.

The tiger cub was taken in by the goats and raised to speak their language, eat their food, and live by their ways. In short, the tiger thought he was a goat.

One day a tiger king was out hunting and came across the flock of goats. The goats fled, but the young tiger wasn't afraid of the tiger king and continued to eat grass. The tiger king asked the young tiger what he was doing posing as a goat, but the young tiger was only able to bleat in response.

The tiger king picked him up and carried him to the water, where he forced him to look at their reflections side by side. For the first time, the young tiger saw his face. The tiger king said, "Look. Look at us. We are the same. You have the face of a tiger!" The young tiger was starting to understand, but only the bleat of a goat passed his lips. The tiger king took him back to his lair and offered him raw meat. At first, the young tiger was repulsed by the taste, but slowly it warmed him. His body woke up, and the truth became clear.

Spontaneously, the young tiger lashed his tail, held his head back, and gave a mighty roar. He knew who he was.

Awareness allows you to take a closer look at yourself and open yourself up to who you really are and who you want to be. Will you be a tiger or a goat?

I have used these steps and every single tool and practice outlined in this book to move me back to my true self and activate living from radical self-love. Am I perfect at it? No, but I also don't expect to be. I am compassionate with myself. The magic of life is the thrill of twists and turns. With awareness and radical self-love, it's easy to navigate that windy stream, and when obstacles or curveballs come my way, I am able to move around them with ease and hit some home runs! My positive qualities have grown exponentially, and I live a higher-frequency life. I am mindful and continue to use affirmations and positive, loving self-talk. *I am the captain of my ship.*

"I deeply love and accept myself."

"I am perfect as I am."

"I am important to myself and the world."

I want to leave you with this, just like me, **you have everything inside you that you need to reach radical self-love**. Your desire and curiosity will be your fuel. No two journeys to radical self-love are the same, and it's perfect to take small steps forward or make a giant leap. However you do it, know that you can clear the way to put yourself first so that your life flourishes. Doesn't that sound good? Your life will flourish. You can give yourself the same care and attention you give others and prioritize self-care. Nurture yourself. And if you get overwhelmed anywhere in the process and need help, you are empowered to reach out and get it.

It's never too early and never too late to reach your own heart. It's waiting for you, cheering you on. Live from the heart of your true self, and you will create your incredible, vibrant life by turning the key of radical self-love.

I'll see you there.

Author's Final Thoughts

Thank you for reading this book!

Every day as I move past my refrigerator, I see the inspiring and wise words of my fridge magnet, **"Life begins at the end of your comfort zone."** I hope this book has taken you to the edge of your comfort zone and has allowed you to create a new perspective on what life can offer when you live from a place of care, compassion, and radical love for yourself.

I remind you to **be compassionate with yourself**; be your own best friend. Rome wasn't built in a day, and the journey to radical self-love has no time limit. The only important thing is that you make it to your destination, and as that plucky little fish Dory in *Finding Nemo* says, "Just keep swimming."

You are important to this world; just by being here on Earth makes you special. Remember to shine your light and light the way for others to follow.

Feel free to get in touch with me. I welcome your feedback and your stories. I would love to hear how your journey to radical self-love goes and the impact this beautiful level of self-love has on your life.

If you enjoyed this book, if it helped you in some way, and if you feel compelled, I would love and appreciate a review on Amazon.

If I can be of any help as a hypnotherapist, BLAST trauma practitioner, coach, or meditation and mindfulness teacher, you can connect with me at:

Email: niki@elementalbalance.ca

Facebook: **Radical Self-Love For Vibrant Living** private group

Website: www.radicalselflovebook.com and www.elementalbalance.ca

Download your Radical Self-Love **free BONUS resources** at www.radicalselflovebook.com

Printed in Great Britain
by Amazon